Happily after all

How To Keep Your Relationship Going When You Are Tired of Trying

TO: _____

FROM: _____

*How To Keep Your Relationship Going
When You Are Tired of Trying*

WILLIE MOORE JR.
with Nigel Lewis

WILFLO PUBLISHING

Happily After All

For information contact WillieMooreJr.org

Cover Design and Book Layout by:

- Chayim Usher, Living Hebrew LLC | LivingHebrew.com
- Kantis Simmons, The SIMAKAN Group | KantisSimmons.com

Photography: Michael Moorer | MichaelMoorerPhotography.com

ISBN: 978-0-9984757-0-7

THE MOORES' THANK YOU'S

Family, we have a host of people to thank for this opportunity. We want to thank God the Father for sending Jesus who paid for our debt of sin and the Holy Spirit for leading us and guiding us everyday. We would like to thank our parents Willie and Flora Moore and Victoria Bruce Coulter for always encouraging us to keep going and supporting us in all of our endeavors. Special thanks to Nigel Lewis. You are and amazing writer and we appreciate you. Thanks to Shanita James our assistant and the heart of our business ventures. We love you. Special thanks to Chayim Usher our graphic designer. Thanks for being so creative. Thanks to the genius of Kantis Simmons. We appreciate you stepping up and fully taking us to the next level on this project. We honor and appreciate you man. To our Attorney Heather Beverly, we thank you for protecting our interests with care. Special thanks to all of our spiritual leaders: Dr. Freddie James Clark, Dr. Creflo Dollar, Bishop Dale Bronner, Bishop Flynn, Dwight Stone, Jermaine Greene, Drea Webb, Lady C and Shanae. We can never thank Radio-One enough for all the love and support you have shown to our family. To all our friends, family and fans we honor and appreciate you. Last but not least to our POWER 500 you all are the best and we love and appreciate you!!!

CONTENTS

God...

Family...

Business...

FOREWORD

- What if your relationship was set up to fail before it even started?

- What if everything you think about relationships isn't true?

- What if no matter how hard you try to make it work, your work isn't good enough?

- What if there is no such thing as happily ever after?

I believe that there are two ways to learn: Mentors and Mistakes. I know you're tired of saying, "I'm sorry" or, "I didn't mean to say that." Tired of the anxiety you feel going to work and trying to smile through it, when the truth is your home is so chaotic that it's hard for you to focus. Don't you want to feel appreciated? Why doesn't your mate just get it? Why is it so hard to make them happy? I have good news and bad news. The bad news is you can't change your mate! The good news is you can change you!

At the time of this writing, I have been married for eleven years and I can publicly say that we went through six years of pure hell before our years of paradise. Most people say, "Willie you stuck around for six years not being happy?" My reply is no! I spent six years believing that SHE was the problem because no one told ME the formula. The formula to get results in a relationship. The way to bring the best out of myself and allow my mate to grow at her pace. I know days are long and nights are longer when you are "going through it" in your relationship, but again I have good news. Your relationship will work out, and anything that you can work out can get stronger.

As your suspense rises to find out what the relationship formula is, I want to warn you about something before you jump head first into this book. I'm not some genius who has all the answers. However, I am a person who has humbled myself for the sake of making my family work. And it has worked.

If you are single you will be happy to know that this book can apply to your life as well. During the first six years of my marriage I possessed a single man's mindset, so I can understand and help you in your process to develop the healthy relationship God desires for your life. I encourage you to buckle your seatbelt and enjoy the stories and lessons ahead.

My prayer is that you accept me as your mentor during this process and that something will speak to your heart. I pray you will avoid the mistakes that often destroy a potentially great relationship. So… at the beginning of this I asked you a few questions. Let me ask you those questions again a bit differently…

- What if you could learn how to make every failure in your relationship a learning opportunity so that you can be better for the higher purpose of your relationship?

- What if there was someone who could help you when your "good" isn't good enough?

- What if there was a way for you to live "Happily" after ALL you've been through?

I plan to make these "what if's" a reality for you. Let's dig in!

✳ ✳ ✳

INTRODUCTION

Why Do I Think This Way?

You know, many times in our adult relationships we can look back and see the early childhood influences that are responsible for what we think, the things we say, and sometimes how we act today. When it comes to healthy and unhealthy relationships, who or what we were exposed to in our youth directly affects who or what we expose ourselves to as adults. Keep it 100! When you think about the people in relationships you've had trouble with or are having issues with now, are there some things you just know come from their past? Guess what?... You are no different! Your past relationships, upbringing, and society in general has given you a very narrow perspective of what your expectations are in your relationship.

Ladies, when you were just little girls with your Barbie and Ken dolls and you were playing house, you were already starting to develop ideas about what a man and woman do in a relationship. Fellas, when we watched the hero punch, shoot, and karate chop his way through the bad guys and get the pretty girl at the end, we were already learning what it supposedly meant to be a man. To this day, Hip Hop has played a pivotal role in my thought process of how to treat women. The great Snoop Dogg said "B****'s ain't s*** but hoes and tricks", and if you listened to that song as a kid you probably had a hard time trusting women. As an early teen you probably had your favorite television shows with people who walked and talked like you. I know for a fact that shows like Martin, The Cosby Show, and other television programs shaped a huge portion of my thought process of what a healthy family unit looked like. These shows were presenting Hollywood's idea of love and relationships. Nowadays you are all grown up and on social media or busy watching reality TV, where relationship advice is coming from every angle and often times the advice is being given through a filter of fiction. If you're not a housewife of a certain city or town, if you're not making millions of dollars, if you can't buy a 10 karat ring for your wife, if you can't spend a trillion bucks on a wedding, then you can't be in a good relationship. REALLY? This is what today's mainstream media portrays as a healthy relationship and this is adding unnecessary pressure on you. I have a really applicable solution for this pressure, CUT IT OFF! That's why these tell-lie-visions and not so smart phones have off switches. #FLATOUT

I can remember when we were losing our home (as well as the cars) and we were in a financial crisis. My wife would choose to still watch what I have coined "Smut TV." Every time she would get off the couch after watching I could almost feel the pressure. She would get on the phone with her friends and talk about the shows and about what she wished she had. She wasn't doing it intentionally but it really bothered me. For me it said "What you're doing isn't good enough." Because of that, strife built up in our relationship and it took years to get over. And all that time I had the power to simply turn the television off or inspire her to turn it off.

I have compiled some of the best stories of our marriage that I know for a fact are going to entertain you, enlighten you, and prayerfully change your relationship for the better. When you discover that you are not alone in the fight for a good relationship, I believe you can stick it out and pass this test you're in right now. Even God said it wasn't good for man to be alone. Loneliness comes in more than one physical form. It's easy to feel alone when nobody is keeping it real with you, so I'm letting the cat out of the bag... Every day isn't a good day and relationships are real work that require a real strategy and plan. I know sometimes you feel like you're the only one that feels unappreciated, the only one going through financial turmoil, the only one who feels less than a man, the only woman who is putting all of herself into her family while nobody notices. Again, I have good news for you. YOU ARE NOT ALONE! God has sent this book to add a fresh perspective to your relationship. See, if you only knew that those same people smiling on social media had a horrible argument minutes before the red carpet, you would feel more at peace about the mishap you had right before church because your husband was rushing you out of the house (You know I'm right about itit). We have more in common than we think, so I invite you to take your mask off and be free with this book. You will have some "Honey, read this!" moments in this book. Some "I can't believe they went through all of that!" moments in this book. You may even look at your mate and say "Baby, compared to them we are not that bad." If that's the case, we ain't mad at you. I challenge you to turn off the phone and television so you two can get better, starting with your foundation.

I grew up as the adopted son of two great, loving parents. I watched them work, buy a house, and retire. I built my ideas of what relationships meant by watching these two people in and around that household. My wife Patricia, on the other hand, is the product of a single parent household. Her ideas on healthy relationships were based on her mom, along with her aunt, and the other people surrounding her as she grew up. We were from two very different backgrounds, but neither of us had a perfect concept of what a relationship should be when we were married. What we had was what we all have… a foundation.

So many people build new relationships based on the foundation of their youth without ever checking to see if that foundation is solid enough for a new relationship to stand. If you didn't grow up in a healthy household those defective bricks play a role in your foundation. When a builder begins the construction of a new home project, they focus on making sure the foundation is good and sturdy. They don't spend as much time worrying about décor and design, because they know nothing can be built up if that foundation has cracks and is unable to support the weight. There will also be an inspection to determine if this building is safe for living. We need to inspect each other's foundations the same way! Can they support the weight of pressures that are sure to come? Are they safe for living? If not, we need to clear away the foundations made up of broken ideas and poor role models and begin to build all new foundations for our relationships.

I don't want it to be a surface conversation either. Dig

deep! Not just, "How many kids do you want?... Where do you want to live?... What kind of car do you want?" Those are good questions, however, I am talking about digging in like, "What's your credit score today?... Do you have any outstanding debt that needs to be handled before we get to deep in this thing?... Are you secretly gay?... How many people have you slept with?... Are you HIV positive?... What is your stance with JESUS?" I always encourage people to have a good fight and see who that person becomes. Do they bounce back easily or do the hold a grudge? See what she looks like without the makeup and the weave before you get too deep. A good hair unit install can have a man fooled until he wakes up with a woman with a Mohawk and one eyelash. Just keepin' it 100! This is your life, and forever is a long time, so why not be bold and find out the truth so you can build your foundation correctly.

I wrote this book to help guide couples and families in their search for better communication and understanding when it comes to developing healthy relationships. Again, I'm not a genius in this area, but I promise to be open and honest in sharing the lessons I believe are the keys to success and the mistakes I've learned to avoid as a result of doing it wrong. All I ask is that you stay committed to doing the work by having tough conversations when necessary, praying for help throughout the process, and finishing the book. I believe the steps contained in these few chapters will help you win in your relationship.

MY PRAYER FOR YOU

Father, I pray that You would open the mind and the heart of the person reading this book. Let them be receptive and undistracted while reading these chapters. Father, You have put my wife and I through so much so that we can be a blessing to the person reading this book. I declare that life will never be the same; life will change for the better. IN JESUS NAME! AMEN

* * *

Me as a "New Creature"

OH MY GOD!

Chapter 1

Now I grew up in church, but I didn't grow up "churchy" if you know what I mean. Some of you may have been like me and went to church every Sunday with your auntie or your grandmother, but it wasn't like my mama and daddy were going religiously (more to the point, you better believe Willie Moore Sr. could preach you under the table with that Word any day, but he just never "did church" like that), so it was an option for me growing up. Patricia didn't grow up like that. She knew ALL of the hymns, went to Sunday School, Sunday Service, and Bible Study. Patricia grew up "in the church."

Honestly, as a boy I enjoyed church. Friendship Missionary Baptist Church in St. Louis Missouri was our little "family" church in the neighborhood where the Rev. Herbert Becton served as Pastor. I was an usher and I was in the choir. I clearly recall patiently waiting to play the piano and the drums after church because even then I loved instruments and music. I really loved my Pastor. I just can't remember any of his sermons. Not that they weren't any good, but I was a child and I didn't understand the big words. I knew he was an amazing man and I honored him because he was such a loving person. I remember when he would sing that high musical note near the end of his sermon. I knew immediately that the altar call was coming. Once those one or two souls came up for salvation, I was minutes away from my time on the piano and drums. Hallelujah! As a matter of fact, when I first began in ministry I felt overwhelmed when people would come in large numbers to the altar. I knew I didn't say anything THAT GREAT (I almost cussed one time), so it had to be Jesus. I had just never seen that in our small family church because most of the patrons were actual members of the church and we all had given our lives to the Lord. So when it came to knowing the culture and the protocols of church, it wasn't like I was some heathen, but… I was NOT the one to look to.

When Patricia and I started dating we were not on the same page when it came to church. For me church was a negotiable option, but for her it was non-negotiable. If I took her out on a Saturday and we came in late, no matter what the time or how tired we were, I could not get her to chill on a Sunday. It was non-negotiable… Patricia was getting up at 8:30 to go to church.

I'd say, "I know you're hungry 'Tricia… Let's go grab something to eat or whatever."

"No. I gotta go to church." she said.

We could come in at 4 a.m…. Sit and talk until 5-6 a.m… and she would still be ready at 8:30 a.m. to go to church.

"Where you going…? Chill!.. I'm not going to be here every Sunday. Church will be there. We can go next Sunday!"

"I gotta go to church."

I'd be on three or four hours of sleep at best when she would return refreshed with her Bible and notes from the sermon, face bright and excited. I mean she actually looked like she was beautified from the experience!

"I'm ready now," she said. "I'm ready."

"What are we ready for?" I was confused.

"The week. I'm ready now."

She looked like she was ready for battle when she came home. I mean like that look on football players faces when they come running out of the tunnel.

"What was y'all doing at church? This is crazy!"

I had never seen anyone come from church this different! I was amazed that I went to sleep and woke up hours later, but she had more energy than me. I had to see what was going on at this church. So I went. And Oh- My- God! This dude was preaching and teaching on things that were REAL TO ME. Things like sex, drugs, mercy, grace, and love! WOW! It was great, to say the least. His name was Pastor Freddie James Clark from Shalom Church City of Peace. He came from the northside of St. Louis and had a street upbringing. Although he had the deep baritone voice that most Pastors I'd heard had, he had a fresh perspective and love for those who didn't have it all together. I still don't know how week after week he was able to tailor a message that spoke directly to me, but through God he did. Later, I found out that no matter where you are, God sits high and He loves us not because we are so good but because He is so good. I thank God daily for using Pastor Clark! As I recall he said, "This is not a body of perfection, it's a body of process." I thought- "Oh, he's 100. THIS IS REAL." I got up when he had the altar call, and Patricia's reaction was as if she had been waiting for SO LONG. She screamed and cried like a baby. I can remember thinking, "Was I that bad?" After long years of feeling like I wasn't good enough because of my smoking, drinking, cussing, pornography and other sins, that day I gave my life back to God.

Now the church happened to sit in the middle of my childhood neighborhood. As I was leaving the church I looked through the large window with rain running across the glass panes. I glanced out and had a glimpse of my troubled past. I saw the little blue house across the street. That was the house where my friend Cee lived with his grandmother. I remembered times sitting there in a car with him and a sack of crack rocks while he sold drugs right across the street from the church where I was now re-dedicating my life to God. Literally, I could stand in the church and look out the window at my past, then turn to look at the altar and see my future. WOW!

See, because my wife was strong in her convictions when it came to church, she was able to assist in saving my life. Don't get together with someone and change your foundation. Some people are so in a rush to meet their Mister or Misses Right that they give up everything in the process. I'm not saying you can't meet on level ground, because all relationships are give and take, but the process of building a relationship is like building a house. You can give away the shutters, change the windows out, strip the siding away, but you don't give away the foundation. The things that make you...YOU.

Being a man, it's sometimes tough for us to take orders and instruction from anyone, including a Pastor. Some of us still see Pastors as authority figures who are flawed like us. So, how can they tell us what not to do and what to do? That may seem strange to you, but these are the thoughts that go through our head. Every man wants to be in power and the Pastor is powerful. That's why you sometimes see people branching off to start churches without order. Often somebody is having a power struggle. With that being said I want you to be mindful of how gentle and prayerful you have to be for your mate to get in the walls of the church. Many people have been hurt by church people and still have wounds that they don't even remember they have, so they don't go to church anymore. Maybe you fall into this category, so I would like to publicly apologize for everything that's been said or done in church that may have hindered you from a true relationship with God. In your relationship you are going to need a common denominator, a referee, a standard to defeat the woes of the enemy's attack on your union. That standard is God's Word. The practice field is church, and life…. well, that is the "LIVE GAME" and I want you to win the championship! #FLATOUT

When you read this story I know all of the ladies are getting a pep in their step as they get ready to go to church now. Please understand that it wasn't the fact that my wife was going to church, it was the fact that church was actually coming home with her. Ladies, I challenge you to come home different than you were before you left. When you come home just as mad, mean and upset as you were before you left - we see no need to go. It's easier to stay at home and watch the football pre-game. I didn't admire the church because of anything she was saying, but because of what I was seeing. Her approach was different. I was able to follow her lead to church because after a crazy week she was determined to make it to this place that promised her a chance to be refreshed and renewed. That was attractive to me.

See, no matter what your mouth says the proof is in the pudding. When your walk is doing the talking you can actually be quiet. Jesus said that they will know us by our love. Not by the shiny cross around our necks or what church we attend, but by the love we show to one another. If you can't love your mate and show him or her the love of Christ, you are doing a disservice to the body of Christ and to be honest - you are making God look bad. #FLATOUT

ASSIGNMENT

If your mate is not a church-goer and you desire for him or her to go; I am challenging you to be consistent in your "Christ" walk. Walk in love by any means necessary. It takes two people to argue, so if an argument is coming, I challenge you to be quiet until you can represent the Kingdom in love.

SAY THIS PRAYER WITH ME

Father, I know that You have given me the authority to defeat the enemy. Father, I pray that You would give me full wisdom on how to execute my authority in heated situations. Father, I desire to see my mate in a healthy relationship with You because it's Your desire that none of us perish. Father, I want him/her and I to enjoy the church experience together, not separately. God, I thank You for giving me the strength to not only hear the Word but to be a doer of the Word. I know that You will give me Kingdom influence in my home and as I pray I believe You have worked it out. IN JESUS NAME! AMEN.

✳ ✳ ✳

1. Make sure that you bring church home. Meaning, you are displaying your change. I'm not asking you to be fake. I'm asking you to yield to the loving response in every situation.

2. Don't nag him/her about church. No one likes to be bullied. Pray about your timing of invitations and continue to be prayerful that God would soften your mate's heart.

3. Make sure that you are consistent with your walk. If you go to church on Wednesdays and Sundays, make that your non-negotiable. People buy into urgency and consistency. If you have an urgency for God's house, your mate will see that and in God's timing, He will compel them also.

Family, I love you so much and so does God. I know that a good church home is going to strengthen you more than you can ever imagine. Be patient with your mate and consider the inner struggles they may be going through and love them through it like God does for you.

Love you,
Willie Moore Jr.

"SEE, NO MATTER WHAT YOUR MOUTH SAYS THE PROOF IS IN THE PUDDING. WHEN YOUR WALK IS DOING THE TALKING YOU CAN ACTUALLY BE QUIET."

Me and Baby Khalil
(My Firstborn Son)

BABY MAMA

Chapter 2

Now, I am NOT in support of sex out of wedlock, although by the title of this chapter you may have figured out that I've had some. I didn't think it would ever catch up with me, but it did. I don't know why God likes to reach me through people over the phone, but He does. I can remember getting the call. I was on the balcony of our condo in Galveston, Texas during Kappa Beach Week. I was mentally preparing for a show in Mississippi on that weekend when the phone rang.

"Willie, I'm pregnant."

"Congratulations!" I said. "Who's the daddy?"

"You."

Please remember, this was Pretty Willie on the call. I actually thought, "Oh, she ain't gonna have it." I thought for a moment more and then I asked, "Cool. What are you going to do?"

Even now as I write this I can't believe how nonchalant I was about the option of aborting a child. That's just how confused I was at that time in my life. I know now that children are a gift entrusted to parents from God for His glory, no matter how they come into the world, but back then... "What are you going to do?" was what I knew.

She made it clear that she was going to have this baby. At the time I was dating another young lady and this news brought that relationship to an end. That hurt me a lot because this woman was my everything at the time. I was just a young man listening to Hip Hop music and I thought having multiple women was the thing to do. Besides, that's what *Bishop* Tupac Shakur and *Bishop* Notorious B.I.G. taught us. Once the baby was born, I tried to make things work with the mother of my child, but my growth process in the area of relationships was a little too slow for her to deal with. My process included clubs, women, liquor, and money, money, money at the time. Her process was to settle down and live a life of monogamy, love and marriage. That just wasn't on my list of things to do at 21 years old. Still, this baby boy had changed my life. I enjoyed the joy of spending time with him. Even just dropping him off at the daycare was a joy. At the time of his birth I was a touring artist and after my concerts I now looked forward to getting back to him as fast as possible. If we were 12 hours away from my hometown of St. Louis, Missouri I would literally have my team attempt to drive back in the middle of the night so I could see his little innocent eyes when he woke up. I was even determined to be different from my friends who had baby mamas. They often let women they referred to as "aunties" come in and out of their children's lives. As for me, I would not bring random women around my son, despite my lifestyle as a "rapper". There was something about the way he would look into my eyes that just made me want to change for the better. He depended on me, he trusted me and he loved me with no ulterior motives.

Before long, I had changed in many ways because of my love for my son. This included removing curse words from my music because I wanted to set an example for him. I was with Patricia by now, as well. The funny thing is, Patricia made it clear when we met that she was never a fan of men with baby mamas. Not to mention that my son's mother was a popular radio personality in St. Louis and would often say things on air that were personally offensive to Patricia and myself, causing my wife to develop some resentment towards her. So as the middle-man in this I had to deal with two women who were not doing their best at handling the role that the other carried. No matter how they felt about each other I expected a certain level of respect from both, and I made that clear.

As men, we are called to be the leaders of our family. The structure and makeup of that family does not change the responsibility we have been given. One of the things that I have learned over time is that in order to have success, you must have a vision. I desired and prayed for success in my family. The saying is true "You can't choose your family", but you do have the option to write a vision for your family. Once I made the decision that I was going to be with Patricia (after some self-help books or a conversation with my Dad- honestly, I can't remember), I wrote down a vision. The vision for what I wanted my son's life to be like and what I wanted our blended family to look like. I must admit it felt silly writing this mini novel of what I wanted my family life to be, but successful businesses have a business plan and mission statement, so why not mimic what I had learned from business into my family life. Men, we are serious about our careers and handling our business, so we have to be serious about the business of our families just as well.

My vision wasn't "deep" but it went something like this, *"WILLIE... WHAT DO YOU WANT???"*

Mission Statement

1. We will set the example for blended families around the world so that God can get the glory from it.

2. After God, I want to have the most influential voice in my son's life.

3. I want the man that comes into his mother's life to be a man that honors God.Now, I did try to *help* God in the process at times; *i.e.*

if they didn't fit the profile I *helped* them find their way out of the mother of my child's life.

4. I want my wife respected as MY WIFE and my son's mother respected as THE MOTHER OF MY CHILD.

This meant acting as a filter by answering questions like, "Who is she to you?" or "Is that coming from you or from her?" It also meant correcting either of them when they spoke disrespectfully toward the other, because ultimately the respect wasn't initially about one honoring the other as much as it was about making sure my son was the common interest. That interest was going to be built on respect. I have to admit to you that sometimes it was hard, but I stood my ground and stayed true to the vision I'd created through God for my family. Respect is big to me. This filtering went on for the first 6-7 years of my son's life, but I had my plan and my vision and I was sticking to it. I felt like God was leading me despite what things looked like in the natural. 6-7 years is a long time to wait for that vision, but I did. And in the end it worked out! It worked out so much so that my wife ended up doing the makeup for the mother of my child's wedding. Hallelujah!!!

Wait!

Don't start dancing just yet- We still have our issues with money and the cultural differences of two totally different home dynamics, but all in all we have a constant growth and a healthy blended family. God has a plan... and... A SENSE OF HUMOR.

The Man Baby Mama Married

My son's mother married a man who did not understand our relationship in the beginning. I couldn't believe it. I'm looking at him like, "I prayed for you!" Yes, this was a man who honored God, (like I prayed for) but he'd had a blended family too, and my vision for my family looked a little *different* from the family dynamic he was used to. The mother of my child and I have disagreed at times, but for the most part we are good parenting partners for our child. You can find us laughing and talking about our son... which is healthy, right? I respect the mother of my child. I go shopping with my son and the mother of my child and instead of having strife with her I've always attempted to find the good in her and in our situation.

While she was dating the man who would become her husband, the mother of my child told me that he was having a difficult time understanding our family dynamic so we couldn't talk as much. I respected her for standing her ground and doing what she felt was best for her new relationship. There was only one thing I could do. Whelp! It was time to have a conversation with the man I had prayed for to come into our lives. He was now an active part of our family's life. I didn't come right out and say "I heard you had a problem with me and my baby mama relationship!" Of course not! Men are easily offended and as I told you before, I am big on respect. In a conversation we were having about something totally different, in a roundabout way, I told him that I didn't desire to have any other type of relationship with his woman besides a healthy parenting relationship. I loved her as the mother of my child, nothing more-nothing less. She is a good friend and I would never cross the line... EVER.

Side note: Fellas it's important that you don't ever go back to the baby mama's cookie jar if you are not going to be with her. That only complicates the blended family process.

From that point on he and I have been great dads to our son and friends to each other. Can you believe that I talk to him more than I talk to her sometimes? He is a Pastor and a prophet of God. (*True Story: Before God blessed me with the radio opportunity he called me and told me that God was about to put me on the radio so I should get ready*). He is almost like a big brother to me and on those occasions when I shut down and don't wanna talk with his wife about something, he encourages me to talk to her. To my son he is the "other dad", because we don't do "step dads." This man puts food on the table, attends games, listens to my son's problems, and he also keeps his house thriving. So that isn't "step parenting" that's being a daddy. #FLATOUT! It's safe to say I love them both and despite the minor debacles, we are making it work.

 **Our Blended Family**

IF YOU'RE IN A BLENDED FAMILY,
SAY THIS SHORT PRAYER WITH ME:

Father, I have gotten myself in a situation that I know may not be pleasing to You, but I know it comes as no surprise to You. I pray that You would give me a vision for my family dynamic so that I can have a goal. Father, I know that You aren't mad at me. I know You are mad about me, so I humbly come to You asking for wisdom. I know that You have the answers. So Father, I am requesting that You would train me to stay focused on what's best for the child and not my personal selfish wants. Children come from You and I honor You for trusting me with a child. I submit my plan to You and I believe it will succeed. IN JESUS NAME! AMEN

✳ ✳ ✳

Remember ladies, even though you are not the woman in your child's father's life it's important that you put on your grown woman panties and be respectful to whoever's next. As long as she is not hurting your child or polluting your child's mind you have no say so on how they run *their* household. If anything happens that you don't like, you go to your child's father <u>first</u> because it's his job to handle the issues in his home! Seek God by praying for the right words to say. *Never*, I repeat **never**, have a conversation with him while you are at the peak of your anger. He is not like other guys you've had in your past. You have to know him in some capacity for the rest of your life. Words can hurt a man although he won't say it. Choose your words wisely! Lastly, please refrain from speaking negatively around your child in regards to your child's father. Being in the car speaking to your girlfriends about what's going on in your life is not a good idea. Always be aware that little ears are listening. Stay in the race. You too should write a vision of what you would like to see happen in your family dynamic so when God blesses you with "Boaz" you have something to explain to him about your current family dynamic. All men respect a woman with a plan.

Brother…

You have a tough road ahead of you because in your mind you can think of some dead-beat dads who chose not to do anything for their children. You feel like you are doing wa-a-a-a-ay more than any other man you have seen. Can I tell you that I applaud you for being more than what you have seen in your past, however, you can't be a dad for a pat on the back. You have to be a dad because God chose you to be. What people don't appreciate on earth God sees in heaven and there is a reward for you. When you have two women in your life, sometimes it will feel like you are being a referee. But never put down your whistle and never stop communicating. You have your plan written down now, (don't you?) so it's important that you hold your wife/ fiancé in high regard in the eyes of the mother of your child. Never discuss the woman who shares in your intimacies, arguments, and disagreements with the mother of your child. She's your parenting mate - not your shoulder to cry on. You can't give her mixed signals because that will complicate things. Fight the good fight of faith. Out of all the people in the world remember… God chose **YOU** for this moment. Remember your child shouldn't have to suffer because of what happens to you and the mom. Stay in the race and don't quit!!!!

I Love You Family, #FLATOUT
Willie Moore Jr.

"DON'T EVER GO BACK TO THE BABY MAMA'S COOKIE JAR IF YOU ARE NOT GOING TO BE WITH HER."

A Pretty Willie Performance

WHERE DEM DOLLARS AT?

Chapter 3

One of the biggest challenges to any relationship is... (DRUMROLL PLEASE) - MONEY. When Patricia and I first started out I was making some and she was making some. So naturally, we thought like the world teaches us to think. My money was my money... and her money was her money. Period. All of that come together, joint account stuff?...UH-UH- NO-NO. I was never a believer. My wife and I did have tough conversations about money early on, but they weren't tough enough. In my mind I had MY condo and she had HER condo. She had a job; I had a job. I liked shopping and well, she liked shopping a whole lot more. I just wasn't ready to join the "OUR MONEY" ministry like that and she wasn't either.

Mistake number one was that I did not do a good job of explaining my money situation. The bulk of my income at the time was shows and cd sales. In other words, the club was my main source of income. I made between $5,000-$10,000 every time I did a Pretty Willie date. Little Rock, Memphis, and Jackson were really popular cities where I could get the big bucks. My wife only saw the end of the process back home in St. Louis, not the grind of hopping city to city that created the money being spent. After all of our travel expenses, hotels, liquor, clothes, jewelry… and you gotta pay the homies, right? Right! I would usually come home free and clear with about $5k-$7k. Not bad for a B-List artist on the road consistently working every weekend.

Then I got saved and everything began to change. For some reason the club and my new self were not seeing eye to eye with each other. Nobody told me to stop clubbing and making money, it was just that something on the inside of me was changing and I could not ignore what was happening. Pretty Willie made his last club appearance in Memphis, Tennessee. The line was wrapped around the corner when I pulled up. You have to understand that we didn't receive any play on radio in Memphis, but at the time Myspace was the main influencer for all teens and it just so happened I had the #1 song on Myspace. This was a $3000 advancement *and* a door split. There had to be 3,000 people at $20-$50 per person in the building. Can you say PAY DAY!

We pulled up in the Ford Excursion and the team was excited. In some cities only a few hundred people would show up, but tonight was different. We were at the peak of our game. We had a record deal, we had plenty of money; plenty of influence - but I was changing.

"You Ready Champ?" my manager asked.

I smiled and said "Yes!"

I heard the DJ say, "Y'all ready to see Pretty Willie? Make some noise!"

It sounded like a SEC football game in that club. I had them turn all the lights down. I walked onstage and the music started. The lights came on and the ladies went crazy! The smoke filled room was packed with little dresses and beautiful hair styles. And even though I was an R&B guy the hood respected my ties to the streets, so all the dope boys came out. It felt good to get so much love in a city 45 miles away from my alma mater Ole Miss. I knew something was going to happen that night. I had one song in particular that was a big hit in the south called "Lay Yo' Body Down!" and that night when I sang it, it felt different. Usually when it came on I got happy because no matter what *that* song would demand attention and the crowd would go wild. Tonight was no different, but I was watching the crowd when "Lay Your Body Down!" came on, and the sight of all those kids dancing sexually to my music stopped me in my tracks.

For the first time the Lord showed me the ugly side of what I was doing. After the concert I was pushing every woman's lustful hand away. I didn't want to be touched or propositioned for sex. I knew I wasn't where I was supposed to be anymore. That night I left the club and entered the hotel lobby where fifty or sixty beautiful women were waiting to be chosen to go back to the room with myself and the entourage. I slipped in through the back only being spotted by a few people. Then I slipped into the elevator and scurried to the room. My bodyguard always pushed four or five different floors so people downstairs could never guess what floor I was on. I reached my room, fell to my knees, prayed and cried. I mean I cried like a baby. This was it! I was done and I had no idea how I would make it financially because this was all I knew (so I thought). A few months earlier I'd heard a voice after a show at the House of Blues in Los Angeles saying "Your way or my way." I knew God was tugging me in a new direction. At that moment I'd made the decision to live for God, but when the bills and the pressure to pay them came I had to get on the road and grind the best way I knew how. The Memphis encounter with God was different. I'd seen my negative influence on teens with my own eyes. The club and Jesus did not go together anymore. I mean, I literally went from being in the HOUSE OF BLUES in Los Angeles to the HOUSE OF THE LORD, OVERNIGHT! Of course, no more sex songs meant a serious hit to my finances. I really felt compelled not to go back to the club unless I came on my own terms, so I was in church going broke with no plan in sight to fix my situation.

Back then I wasn't smart enough to understand that in order to grow in an area, you have to upgrade your relationships and change your surroundings. Whenever you get to a place in your life where you feel like you are hitting a glass ceiling, in my opinion, it's time to level up your friend game and change your surroundings. Adding new information through adding new people to the circle will add new options for growing in your thought process and it will account for diversifying your life portfolio. If you refuse to prepare yourself for success by surrounding yourself with the people who can help you to reach the next level, don't be surprised if you continue running in circles spiritually, physically, and financially. That was a lesson I had not learned yet. No one had told me that God is the greatest planner.

Now I was in a position that was… *different.* I mean VERY DIFFERENT! I had refused to join the "OUR MONEY" ministry and now my wife was the breadwinner.

Side Note: Ladies when a man is not making any money and he can't get on his feet try your best to encourage him or just stay out of the way.

I'm used to making thousands and now I'm lucky to get 'A' THOUSAND. I was in my nice condo living under constant anxiety. I found out financial stress has a voice. For me it would repeat the same phrase over and over. "WHERE DEM' DOLLARS AT THO'?" The end of the month came and Patricia paid OUR car notes, OUR bills, and MY child support. That was a knock to my ego and my identity as a man. I know you see men who are lazy and choose not to do anything for their family- but that's not me. I desired to provide for my family, I just had quit my day job because of the call on my life. Real men take care of their family and provide for them. The exception being that the two of you decide it is better for the man to stay at home with the kids being an awesome dad. That's fine! But that was not the case for us. I was slipping into depression. So to snap out of it I would be at home cooking and cleaning, trying to contribute, but still hearing that voice asking "WHERE DEM' DOLLARS AT THO'?" I don't know if it's because Friday is a regular payday, or if I was just tripping, but I sure felt like leaving *every* Friday. I mean *every*, *every*, Friday I wanted to break up. I stayed, of course, and my thoughts of a break up were replaced with a breakthrough.

While I was praying for advice from my new financial planner JESUS, (I still had a Black and Mild cigar in one hand with a Bible in the other) I got instructions. He showed me through my anxiety and frustration, that a man still has to act like a man even when he is not producing like a man should. *A MAN STILL HAS TO ACT LIKE A MAN, EVEN WHEN HE IS NOT PRODUCING* (Just imagine that in the voice of God). I needed to make sure that I continued to cater to my wife and act like a breadwinner, even though my wallet didn't reflect it at the time. It began with a vision and a plan. It *began* with 'A' vision and 'A' plan. Then it went to two visions. Then three. My plan kept changing and I kept telling Patricia. I was going to do an album. No - I was going to be a public speaker. I had an idea for a clothing line. It went on and on until one day the woman said, "WHAT ARE YOU *DOING?*!!"

I want the fellas to understand that women love stability, but more importantly women need to know that the man in the relationship *knows* where he's going. So when you are the one at home not making any money, it's great to be creative with all of your dreams and visions and plans, but until you can focus on that one thing to share with her and follow through, you need to write it down and SHUT UP! That's right! Shut up, hush and zip yo' lip if you have to! Too many visions is confusing to a woman. She wants to support you, and she wants to see you succeed, but she just can't do confusion. While you are figuring things out don't "boss up" like you have it all together. Be real with your woman and let her know what you are thinking of doing. Don't come in with an attitude of it's already done, because your woman can help if you allow her to be a part of your process. Allow yourself to be vulnerable with your mate and watch how much more fulfilling things will be. I made a decision to start doing funny, inspiring YouTube videos and as crazy at it sounded to everyone I stayed consistent. After months of consistency she knew I was serious and she was able to catch the vision and walk alongside of me.

I want the ladies to know… A man can get through this process but not while you degrade him. I credit my wife with handling me in a loving way through it all. She always treated me like the man she knew I could become. She acted as if she knew one day Willie would be a success on radio, television, speaking, music, *and* that I would be writing this book. Even with me at home, asking "WHERE DEM' DOLLARS AT THO'?" I honor her for NOT listening to the friends and family that were telling her, *"Girl, what he gon' do with his life? You can't just be taking care of no grown man!"* Today she doesn't have to work a 9 to 5 unless she wants to because she supported me against all odds. She married me and not her family. (We will talk about that a little later.)

I said earlier that money is one of the biggest challenges in relationships. If that is the case for you, ask this question-

"Will it fix the problem if I push away my partner, and alienate the person who is supposed to be beside me to face the challenge?"

We have to remember that placing blame and fighting out of frustration is never the answer. The challenge has to be faced together. In my mind I always say, "I don't need your membership or your friendship, I have my wife." What I mean is that our relationship as a team is greater than any outside group, job, opportunity, or person that would come in to separate us or influence us against one another. Don't allow separation to come from the inside. You two are like a 3-strand cord and you are not easily broken. When things go financially haywire make sure you get closer. There's power in agreement. In fact, my favorite book says that if two or more gather in My name there I am in the midst. And if God is in it when you two come together that means you can make it.

ASSIGNMENT

If finances are your biggest issue, I am encouraging you to know that we have unlimited resources in heaven and God desires to get those resources to you here on earth for His glory! Notice I said for HIS GLORY. How can God get the glory in the area of your finances? Believe it or not, in the toughest times we tithed on time and gave offerings to our local church even when we didn't understand how we would make it. BUT GOD! Yes, he stepped in and stretched our little and made it more than enough. GOD WILL PROVIDE!

Remember: *You* have the power of the true and living God inside of *you*. You all have untapped creativity that can only be revealed when you get together and brainstorm on where you are, where you want to go, and how you are going to get there.

Create Vision Boards

Get a collective vision of where you both want to go collectively. Discuss how you are going to get to your destination together. Make sure you find great ministries to sow into. (Don't just sow your seed anywhere. Make sure you give to ministries and causes that represent an area you want to see fruit in. We give to St. Jude, our local church, our home church, and a few television ministries because they represent where we want to go.)

Don't Commit Financial Adultery

Some people have hidden accounts; hidden credit cards. I know this isn't you. It's going to take some real trust to get out of a tough financial situation but you can do it. Be truthful and work together. Make a budget and go over every penny earned and spent once a week and have and extensive meeting at the top of the month.

Find A Scripture To Stand On For Your Relationship

Meaning, a word that speaks to you and your situation. Here's our secret - Google: What does *God* say about finances? I'm serious. Find one that you would like to build your financial future on. If He said it, it will come to pass. Put that scripture on the mirror and read it together every day at some point.

SAY THIS SIMPLE PRAYER

Father, I know that You desire to do me good. I know that there is no lack in heaven and I believe since I am not only a visitor on earth, but also a resident of heaven that there is no lack in my life. You have given me the wisdom to get wealth and You said that the blessings of the Lord maketh one rich and adds no sorrow to it. I believe we are the head and not the tail, above and not beneath and we are faithful with what we have now and expect more tomorrow. IN JESUS NAME! AMEN

* * *

Family, this is not a sprint; it's a marathon. The only time you start off on top is when you're digging a hole. A small step is still a step. Work together and obtain financial freedom.

Love you Family,
Willie Moore Jr. #FLATOUT

"LADIES WHEN A MAN IS NOT MAKING ANY MONEY AND HE CAN'T GET ON HIS FEET TRY YOUR BEST TO ENCOURAGE HIM OR JUST STAY OUT OF THE WAY."

My First Group

I CHEATED

Chapter 4

Those of you who have shared in my journey from YouTube to television, on the radio, and now this book, know that in my "past life" I went by the name Pretty Willie. If you are new to team Willie Moore Jr. I welcome you to the team. Before the lights, camera and action for the Kingdom of God I was a successful R&B artist for many years. I started in the music business when I was only a child. As a matter of fact, I got my very first record deal back home in St. Louis at the age of 12.

I have always been a creative person and like most young people I was searching for validation from the people around me. However, for me, it goes a little deeper. I struggled with being adopted and the feelings that came with that were hard to communicate at 10 or 11 years old. My family told me that if I could write my feelings down and then look at them, I could really process and understand my feelings better. I didn't know then that my God given creativity would transform those feelings into songs, but when I discovered I could rap & sing and people would validate me through their applause for my songs, Pretty Willie was born.

Fast forward a few years and not much had changed. Yes, I had some money and some fame and all of the things that go along with that. Yes, I was now married. But inside I was still seeking the validation. By now I had been in studios for what seemed like all my life, and the one thing that remained consistent for all those years was my need for a creative sounding board. Someone had to be present and ready to connect to my creative space and provide me the feedback I needed. My songs were like my babies, and everybody wants someone to compliment their baby. I just needed to call someone and play them the song so I could hear them say, "That's a beautiful child". It just so happens that my "babies" were always delivered at around 3 a.m.. Would you believe my wife Patricia was not eager to jump up at 3 a.m. and listen to my music?!! Pretty Willie's music?!

I have to admit, it wasn't her fault. She did have to get up for work the next morning. And I would walk into the house at times and think, "All she wanna talk about is bills, babies, and bulls@#!. What about this music I'm doing?" (Okay, I feel some women rolling their eyes... sorry, that's how I thought at the time). But you have to remember I was told, "If you could write your feelings down and then look at them..." I needed to share those feelings with somebody. So I did what many people do when they feel rejected by their spouse. I went out and got a "FRIEND".

Even though she had to go to work the next morning, and even though it was 3 a.m., my friend would answer the call. She made herself available to entertain my need for validation through creativity. Time and time again she was there to hear the good, the bad, and the ugly of what was being recorded in the studio. She gave me the needed attention I desired so much. What I didn't see happening over time, was that we were building a bond. In my mind at the time, there was no harm and no foul. I thought she was nice… I appreciated her ear for the words and feelings I needed to express… but I truly wasn't trying to build a relationship with her. While I was building songs with her input and she was feeding me ideas, I had no idea that we were developing a strong emotional, yet, real relationship.

With all I had going on at home, I had made a logical but errored decision. I had unknowingly made this "friend" my escape from the real problem, and taken part in an emotional attachment. Instead of my wife becoming my resource for support and reassurance, I had allowed another person to fill that space, and my relationship at home was failing as a result. I mean it when I say we were REALLY ready to call it quits. Then I realized… I NEVER GAVE MY WIFE THE OPPORTUNITY TO BE THERE.

This is the part where the fellas want to say, "But Willie, SHE wouldn't answer the call!" I hear you, fellas. Or "Willie, I don't want to hurt her like that." I hear that too. But understand, we have a bad habit of avoiding that tough conversation. You know, the one where we actually sit the woman down and tell her what she needs to know. The tough conversation that *may* bring some tears, some hurt, some anger, but *definitely* a resolution. It must be a guy thing, because if it were one of the homies or that person at work not getting the job done, we would have words. We would sit them down and have that tough conversation. I'm not saying it will be easy, but consider the alternatives. Having the tough conversation will probably be a BLOW to your relationship… but the repercussion of NOT having the conversation may likely END your relationship.

For me, it started with sitting her down and finishing one statement… "Baby, I'm cheating on you." I was confident enough to tell her that because God had revealed that my marriage was not going to work as long as I had a divided interest. I had already told the other young lady that I couldn't continue our phone calls or any other interaction that was outside of my marriage, so it was not about me getting busted. I wanted a resolution to the real problem. That is, I didn't understand the importance of communicating to my wife that SHE was a *desired* and *required* part of my success. We have to begin to desire and require the person we are in a relationship with to be there as a part of any and everything we want to be successful in. My wife didn't understand how important that 3 a.m. call was to me. That was my "non-negotiable". It was difficult, but she made the effort and sacrifice to do the thing that she knew I needed. I then found out something. My wife had a "non-negotiable" too.

I married a makeup artist, brushes and all. Despite all of my video shoots and television appearances, I have never been a fan of makeup. My high school diploma reads **Ferguson-Florissant School District**. Translation- *WILLIE DON'T DO MAKEUP!* That is until I realized that her non-negotiable was for me to show interest and respect for her work. Her "3 a.m." was for me to know what she was talking about in a conversation involving palettes and contouring. I didn't want to leave any room for my wife to say "I cheated", so I sacrificed and pulled up video after video on YouTube. I paid attention when she talked about her work. I'mma keep it 100… I know something about makeup now. I wasn't gonna let any man step into an intimate space that was meant for me!

The open and honest discussion about our non-negotiable needs allowed us to cut the enemy off at the pass. Things that may have crept in the back door of our relationship before had nowhere to go, because she now knew where I was vulnerable and vice versa, I could take care of her needs too. Because we humbled ourselves and did the work to learn each other's intimate spaces, we left no room for anyone else to fill a void. YOU have to be willing to make it your duty and priority to step into the intimate space of the other person in your relationship. It doesn't matter that you don't like sports, or gardening, or shopping, or whatever that *thing* is. What matters is that you do the work to get to a place where you have their back and they have yours.

Can you imagine what would have happened if Adam had Eve's back and vice versa? Just think, there would have been no place for the serpent to creep in and speak to Eve if Adam was in that intimate space. If Eve had been invited into Adam's intimate space, she may have been too busy helping him with his assignment of tending to the garden and the animals to entertain the serpent. With that being said I would like to challenge you to do some homework.

ASSIGNMENT

If you are in a relationship I ask that you have a tough conversation with your mate. Explain your non-negotiables in a loving way.

WAIT! Before you pick a fight and say the wrong thing…

SAY THESE SIMPLE WORDS WITH ME

God, I need your help to speak in a loving manner to my mate. I love him/her and I want that to be apparent in my tone, in my mannerisms, and in my eyes. God, I have decided that I want my relationship to work and I humble myself right now before You requesting Your peace to rest on both of us. Give me the right words and the right timing to have this conversation. I am leaning on Your Words in Proverbs 15:1 when You said 'A gentle answer turns away wrath', so I pray that my mate is gentle and if he/she isn't I will be. IN JESUS NAME! AMEN

A LOVING WAY…

When having the conversation with your mate please make sure that you always start off with the good. The good may be a compliment or praise for all of the great things he/she is doing. It is important that a person feels celebrated and not just tolerated. Give at least 3 compliments before you go into what needs to be fixed. End the conversation with praise and honor. This is called "THE SANDWICH."

Blessings Your Way,
Willie Moore Jr. #FLATOUT

PATRICIA'S RESPONSE
(I WISH I WOULD HAVE KNOWN)

I came from a world where I was raised to go to school, get good grades, go to college, network, and get a good paying job. "Oh, and make sure you invest and save for your kids and retirement." Anything related to entertainment was a million miles from my grasp or even thoughts. I grew up to be a corporate girl. The American dream was sold to me and embedded in my mind. At the age of 21, I was well into my career as an Auditor which allowed me to travel the 50 states and see different places. Don't get me wrong, there were perks but I had to pay for those perks by putting in the hours.

As I mentioned I was well into the beginnings of my career when I met Willie. Truthfully, I had seen him around town several times. We always bumped into each other at different events (STL is small) however, I was oblivious to who he really was or what he did for work. Until one day I saw him driving in a car that was wrapped with a banner. It had his face and name on it. I was like, "Wow, really?... That's you? That's what's up."

Ok, enough of the back story, let's fast forward to marriage. I had no clue what I was getting into, what was up ahead, or what marriage would require. As my husband stated I came from a single parent home and the only marriage I saw growing up was my Aunt and Uncle who were normal 9 to 5 workers. Therefore, to meet and marry a man in the industry (let alone the music industry) was foreign to myself and my family. The only thing we knew about entertainers was what we saw on TV. Because of that, what I wrote down on my "What I Don't Want In A Man" list was for him not be a celebrity in the forefront, or in the media. That was something I never desired. Growing up without the intimate relationship of a father or experiencing the "Daddy's Little Girl" relationship, I wanted someone who would be an honest and faithful family man. A man who was always involved. Heck, I had in mind the Huxtables' "Cosby Show" fairytale life. That was my only example of what a family man should be.

Now I was a wife with no examples except for the ones I'd seen on TV. All I knew to do was love the way I would want to be loved or treated. I was so clueless of how to love the type of man I married. There was no book, no training, and no guide to show me (or so I thought). Married life was going to be the REAL experience. No more marital bliss; no more honeymoon phase. It was two people from two totally different backgrounds, upbringings, and ideals of what marriage should look like. In the beginning when I felt like I was failing, I was being regular. The regular complaining about keeping the house clean and picking up your stuff. As my hubby would say, "Bills, babies, and BS"! It's what most people are concerned with, right? At the time I had a very demanding job with long hours. Not to mention I was in a career that I really didn't have passion for anymore. Yep, I went to school all those years and found out the career I'd sought after was not what I expected. So with all of that I was just living and not really understanding or paying attention to what my husband needed or wanted.

My hubby was an entrepreneur, a dreamer, and a go-getter. Mr. Hustle Simmons. What he required from me was something I wasn't aware I needed to provide or knew how to give. Man, did this cause a rift in our marriage! Miss Corporate America had excelled at everything in life, but no book smarts could help me pass this test. I struggled! I cried every night because I could feel distance growing between my husband and I and I just didn't understand why.

Then it happened. He told me he was cheating. My heart sank. The one thing I wanted to avoid, the one thing I never wanted to happen, the one reason why before I met him I vowed to stay single and marry the ministry. "Why me Lord?!" is what I thought. What was I doing that was so bad to cause this man to seek a relationship outside the one we had? By no means will I ever blame myself for his selfish actions, but I noticed some things that I could have done better. I wasn't there mentally and physically. I wasn't there in the moments when he needed a friend. Now we were best friends before marriage, but during that time in our marriage it had all changed. Yes, when it was fresh I would stay up late nights talking on the phone and dreaming with my little dreamer until the sun came up (and I'd go to work SUPER tired). That's what happens when you first meet someone new and exciting. The conversations are amazing, right? See I didn't meet Pretty Willie. I met Willie Moore Jr.. The momma's boy, the family man, and the cool dude who almost could be like a brother. He'd shielded his industry life from me and showed me him; His heart. He didn't want me to know about the music business and how crazy it was. He wanted to be himself and I guess, have an escape. However, he still wanted me to be that same escape when we got married.

Now let me say this, when he told me he cheated I thought he was really selfish. How dare you cheat on a woman who is trying to hold it down! Our agreement was he was the risk-taker and I was the stability. He would invest in his career while I keep the consistent job to maintain some kind of foundation in the household. "So how could you do this?!! I'm working tirelessly, thinking this is a way of support!" To him, my working was all good, but he needed his escape. He needed me to sacrifice and stay up late and support his new projects or "babies" as he would label them.

To be honest and truthful ladies, it is almost impossible to continue to do the same things you did in the beginning of your relationship. We all grow amd change, however we should always be an ear for our man if he is willing to share his dreams and be vulnerable with you. Believe it or not, men need more encouragement than we do sometimes. They are afraid at times and don't know how to communicate their fears. They can hear all the good compliments from everyone else but the one pat on the back they really want to receive has to come from us. Men desire our applause and our acceptance.

After Willie's confession we discovered that we never talked about the type of wife he needed, what that looks like, what he desired, and vice-versa. It was not just about what we saw growing up and what we learned from our families in the past. It was about what we needed to build together. What does that look like? I was blessed to marry a man who was willing to seek God and wisdom from mentors; therefore, our first example of what a good marriage looked like had to come from God. This meant we needed to learn to communicate everything. Our most intimate feelings and thoughts. The Come-to-Jesus type of tough conversations that we needed to have first before operating in our feelings and making decisions we knew were temporary, but that would have a lasting effect. We've endured a lot, but it always comes back to "What would Jesus do?! What does the Word say about how we should respond to each other, love each other, treat each other, and thrive in marriage?" Not just LIVE! THRIVE!

**Early Days of The
Young Fly and Saved Crew**

THAT'S JUST YOUR THING

Chapter 5

So business-wise, I believe men and women in general have different attitudes towards how we handle things. There are always exceptions to this of course, but *in general* there is a difference. We (MEN) tend to focus on the thing(s) that we relate to and take on the role of the hunter-gatherer. We see that THING and go after it with 90% of our focus, because that THING will provide for the bills and the bows. You know what the *bows* are ladies... all the things you like that we go the extra mile for to make you happy and comfortable. For instance, in my house I am an active supporter of the SHOE MINISTRY (I hear some of my sisters shouting, *HALLELUJAH*!!). Of course, there is nothing wrong with a man that wants to provide for his family. But, your relationship could be pushed into conflict when you become so focused on handling business that you risk missing milestones in your relationships. Let's talk about it.

Early on, Patricia and I had issues with that THING coming between us. I was this new man, this new version of myself, with

Coach Jesus calling the plays and me running the ball to score for the kingdom. I was knee deep in ministry on YouTube with thousands of followers. I had a fast growing youth service in Tulsa, Oklahoma and the Young Fly & Saved Movement blowing up all over. Plus, I was steadily trying to provide for the bills and the bows at home. I would be busy working on a new sermon, working on a new song, or working on outreach programs… all the time not seeing the look on my wife's face. She had been sitting on the sidelines of my THING and developed a new face and a look that said, "That's just HIS Thing".

I can remember first noticing the new face and that look. Patricia and I were in Tulsa at Greenwood Christian Center preparing for the Women's Encounter. Women from all across the country were coming to this event and at the same time huge numbers of youth were being saved and changed through the Young Fly & Saved Movement. We were active in area churches and schools, while working to influence this young generation. But, for the first two months of my discipleship there I had not brought Patricia with me, only a few members of the YFS team. So based on my energy and involvement there was this excitement about Patricia finally coming to Tulsa for the event.

"I can't wait to meet your wife if she's *anything* like you!"

Patricia came to Tulsa and was met with smiles and love from all of the people our team had worked with in ministry. The

Women's Encounter was a phenomenal event. Women were so excited about what that they were going to take home with them after the life changing experiences from the first day. Later on that night when I was finally able to spend some alone time with my wife, she gave me her honest opinion on how the event had affected her by asking me one question:

"Do I gotta go back?"

(You get so focused on business at times that you miss some things-)

The next day the buzz was already going around the church.

"Willie's wife was just not that into it. She wasn't getting involved."

There was an overall feeling of disappointment from many of the women who were so gung ho about meeting Patricia just the day before. Even worse, some took it as an open invitation to try getting closer to me (Yes, churches have groupies too)! I mean you really could feel a negative energy in the atmosphere that next day. Before day two was closed out, Patricia and I had an argument right there about everything. It got to the point that while I was on stage I actually addressed the issue with the people in the audience. I had to admit to them that I had been spending a lot of time in ministry and not a lot of time at home, and at this time we needed to grow in that area and could use their prayers. I was so upset on the inside and hurt that I had overlooked how my work was having a negative effect on my family.

I know now that we both made the mistake of accepting an attitude of "That's Just *YOUR* Thing". It's not that we were really living apart. We were sharing our responsibilities as parents and we both knew 90 percent of what was going on in each other's lives when I was out of town. That was and is NOT enough. I missed the opportunity of developing a relationship of ministry with Patricia involved. In all that we were trying to accomplish in Tulsa at the time, Patricia and I had left out a major component that would help us to be successful - EACH OTHER!! I learned later from my mentor that your partner has to be a part of your business life in some way when you are creating something new. Creative people are spiritually, physically, and emotionally attached to their vision and goals. **If the vision is not shared, the vision is impaired**. Your business can become like your child. You cannot exclude one parent from raising this child, no more than you would have a marriage with a child and only one parent responsible for their care while the other just stood by and watched. MY ministry, MY music, and MY Young Fly & Saved Movement needed to become

OURS. PATRICIA'S work as a makeup artist and PATRICIA'S decisions at home needed to become OURS. Basically WE needed to start handling our businesses together instead of looking at each other and thinking, "That's Just *YOUR* Thing".

Before you go running gung ho into a business you need to write down the vision for that business and make it plain (see the pattern), then come into agreement with your partner by getting them involved on the ground level. BEFORE you turn your house into hell. I'm not saying that it has to be an elaborate business plan but I am asking you to map it out so that your mate can see what you are doing and where you plan to go. My favorite book (The Bible) challenges us to count the cost to make sure that we are sufficient to finish the job (Luke 14:28). It can even be written in crayon but it is important that you write it down. The key word is *AGREEMENT*. For one thing, the *TIMING* has to be right. I know as men we get into our hunter/gatherer mindset and run to go out and claim that prize to feed the family and save them from starving.

We can be in a rush to save what doesn't need saving. Many times if we took the time to ask our wives what was important to them we would find out that they were not so concerned with the prize we were so focused on. While we are busy running around trying to score as many points as possible, they probably stopped looking at the scoreboard long ago. If we focus so much on putting points on the board we can miss out on the ultimate prize, which is the growth of our relationships. As we watch our businesses grow we should be sharing in the journey and each of the milestones along the way.

Patricia and I did just that. After trying to get her to share speaking events, write books with me, and video blog, fashion was where she finally found her niche. My wife started working in our clothing department and in a short time she began to grow the Young Fly & Saved brand. As the brand grew, I was able to talk to her more about the business and outside of "us" we now shared a common interest that we cared about. It was no longer just Willie's thing. It was the ministry that God entrusted us both with, so it required everyone's participation.

Now that we are stronger and wiser in this thing (Hello Pastor Marvin Sapp!), I make sure that my wife is on the frontline in every area of our business. Before I began to write this book, I made sure to share a written vision with her and ask her permission to begin this journey. We came into agreement on the process that would result in us reaching a new milestone - Willie Moore Jr., "Author". What you have to recognize is that I didn't just wake up one day and decide to write a book. This seed was planted five years before, but we used wisdom through seeking God's *TIMING* and our *AGREEMENT*. When the season for the book was right and WE agreed that this was in line with God's plan for our success, we began.

Side Note: For all my brothers and sisters in ministry. I wasn't aware of it at the time, but when I was in my "That's Just YOUR Thing" mindset, it was very apparent to ministry leaders that I was out of balance at home. They thought I was a fraud because they didn't see my wife involved and silently questioned, "What is he doing at home?". And literally, I wasn't doing anything at home at the time to reflect that I honored the FIRST MINISTRY...HOME.

1. Always take the time to explain the vision of what you are doing even if your mate doesn't appear interested. The last thing you want to happen is that your mate finds out about your vision from others.

2. **Try your best to have your mate repeat what you tell him/her about the vision.** Every time you say something it doesn't mean they heard you correctly. Have them repeat the vision to you. Either reading the vision or repeating after you.

3. Because you are the visionary you may spiritually feel leap years ahead of your mate, but **Be Gentle, Patient, and Calm** when your mate is playing catch up to where you are. Anyone can catch up if you allow them to be themselves and don't force them.

Family, I love you and what you are doing. Remember to serve wholeheartedly without expecting a pat on the back. Enjoy the journey.

Sincerely with Love,
Willie Moore Jr. #FLATOUT

"MAKE SURE THAT YOUR WIFE IS ON THE FRONTLINE IN EVERY AREA OF YOUR BUSINESS."

 **Me with Canton Jones,
one of my great mentors.**

I DON'T BELIEVE IN GOD

Chapter 6

After many nights of going back and forth with my own thoughts and feelings of what to do with my life, I decided it was time to move out of my beloved city of St. Louis, Missouri. I had already lived in Mississippi for 4 years and Los Angeles for about 3 years after a deal I took with Warner Brother Records. My music production team was still in Los Angeles. I didn't have much money and the well of opportunity was quickly drying up in St. Louis. The logical thing to do was to run back to LA.

"Yes, that's what I am going to do", I thought, "GO BACK TO L.A.! Besides, if all else fails, I can work with my production team." One of my dear friends promised I could work on set with him and make about $1500 every week. This would be the perfect way for me to get paid and get discovered. Yes!

That made total sense in my head. So I made the announcement to my wife, "Babe I am going to move to Los Angeles for a while and stack some bread and land a role on TV and when I do, I am going to send for you and the family." She reluctantly agreed and tried her best to support my efforts. We were living in a home that was 3 months behind on mortgage. The bank was fed up and so was I. Patricia and I mutually agreed to leave the home. EVICTED! This means in the midst of all my prayers, my fasting, trying to do the right thing, BAD THINGS STILL HAPPENED! The funny thing is, in my heart I always felt like God was going to make a way but in this case, he didn't. Or so it seemed.

I told my wife "I will pack the house", because I knew seeing all of our assets, our memories, our ups and downs being put into boxes would emotionally drain her. The reality was, our nest was being vacated. It was a solemn time for our family to say the least. I can remember crying and smoking, crying and smoking. Here I am in my mid-20s, with two kids, my beautiful wife, and I am being evicted out of our home. I thought all types of thoughts. Maybe I can go buy some weed and pull a quick power play and get back on my feet; or maybe I can make one more sex song, sell some cds, save the money from that and be cool. Maybe I should hit the club again and make some quick bread and call it a day. None of these ideas felt right in my spirit. Los Angeles was MY decision and I was going to go and make a way. The moment that I got my family settled into my mother-in-law's basement (because that is where we decided to go after eviction), I was catching the first thing smoking out of St Louis to L.A.. So, I put on my fake smiles to be strong for my family and asked my wife to let me take care of ALL the house packing but she refused. On a Tuesday while I was preparing for a men's group that I was leading, I got a phone call.

"WILLIE COME QUICK! TRICIA IS HURT!"

"WHAT?"

"Come to the hospital she is so hurt."

"What happened?"

"A glass cut her…. Her leg is..."

"What the hell happened?", I said.

"A clock… Glass..."

"Put my wife on the phone!", I told her irate friend   telling me the story.

Tricia picked up the phone laughing and she told me that the glass from a clock that hung about 30 feet in the air by our vaulted ceiling fell and hurt her leg. What she didn't know at the time is that she had completely severed her Achilles tendon.

When my wife got on the phone she was laughing and giggling like it was all a joke.

Why the heck are you laughing?", I asked.

She said, "I don't know!"

I rushed to the hospital and wouldn't you know the doctor said she may not be able to walk or run again. REALLY! Come to find out she was in shock when we talked. She was laughing and giggling but once the shock wore off , "AAAHHHHHH!". You could hear her screaming all through the hospital. After she was all stitched up and fixed she had at least six to eight weeks to be off of her feet which meant, NO Los Angeles for me! At least for a while.

Those two months of my wife being off her feet and having to depend on me for everything taught me a lot. I began to really read the Bible and really focus on building a stronger relationship with God through Jesus. God showed me that I was a great talker but not a great doer. In those six to eight weeks I learned to serve my wife. And while I was serving, God started showing me things in his Word like, "The greatest people are people who serve others." I learned so much about myself and God through serving my wife. My YouTube ministry got better and better because I was really hanging out with God and he was giving me so much revelation that the world needed to hear. One day during that time, my Pastor F. James Clark talked about having a King to serve and a Giant to Slay. In that service God showed me my dear friend Canton Jones and I felt compelled to go serve him. I thought, "But GOD, Wait! Canton is not in Los Angeles he is in Atlanta!" I fought and I fought but I felt like after Tricia's two months of healing I would move to Atlanta. Not to be famous or to be discovered, but to serve my friend's ministry.

Family, in order for you to be led by God you have to literally saturate yourself in his Word and in what I call, HIS culture. Every day of my life I get a scripture, some prayer, and I listen to at least 20 minutes of my favorite speakers and teachers. Faith comes by hearing, and hearing by the Word of God. Maybe you have experienced fake people in the Kingdom culture. Please be reminded that as long as *people* have something to do with anything mistakes will be made. In order to lead your family or for you to be led in your family you MUST be able to trust the God in your mate. Trust and submission is an invitation for someone to lead. In order to trust a person, you have to learn to trust the God you both serve.

SAY THIS SIMPLE PRAYER

God, I want to get to know You intimately. I desire to have Your wisdom, Your ways, and I want my will to align with Yours. Lead me to the right scriptures that speak to my situation. Lead me to the right speakers to speak into my life. Give me a hunger for the things of Your Kingdom and the will to hate what You hate. My family depends on me and I depend on You. Lead me Father. IN JESUS NAME! AMEN

✳ ✳ ✳

My wife was confused because I had previously told her I was moving to L.A. and I was now saying God was telling me to go to Atlanta. She decided to stay in St Louis until I got my feet planted in ATL or L.A. or wherever the heck Willie was going. I had to be gentle with her. I mean I did change my mind and when you have nothing financially it is tough sometimes for a woman to see the vision. Especially if you change it- OFTEN. It didn't mean my wife wasn't with me, she loved me, but women are made to be secure and stable (Fellas if you give your woman security and make her feel safe physically, mentally, spiritually, and financially you will discover a new love from what the Bible calls the weaker vessel, your woman). I know she appears tough, but deep inside she's gentle. Since I was determined to make my wife secure I made a new announcement to my family. "I AM MOVING TO ATLANTA!" Once that decision was made, it wasn't long before I had packed my Suburban and was on my way to Black Hollywood aka ATLANTA, GA.

So, I'm in Atlanta. And... I wasn't rolling in money. After stepping out on faith with a savings of about five thousand dollars to make the move, I was in my new "promised land". Even though I had used just about all of that money to get us there. With not much left, we were watching the YouTube ministry slowly start to blow up and were looking forward to what God was going to do next. I was truly excited. I was serving Canton's ministry faithfully every day. Then, one day while I was out in the city serving Canton, my buddy Alvin Williams invited me to an event. Rickey Smiley was launching his new television show. Immediately I asked, "Who's gonna be there?.. Rickey Smiley?..Is Tyler Perry gonna be there?"

Y'ALL KNOW! Put me in a room full of influential people and I will faith my way into SOMETHING! And at the time, I felt like just *maybe* God had a plan for me to be on television judging by the success of my YouTube channel.

I did attend the event. I was meeting and greeting, enjoying the opportunity to mix with new people from different backgrounds. I stepped away to run to the restroom. When I stepped out of the restroom a man stopped me.

"Uh…Whassup? Whassup?.. Don't I know you?" he asked.

I looked at the man, trying to see if I remembered him from maybe music or entertainment. I thought it was possible we might have met before. He was well dressed and had the look of someone with money. The expensive clothes, jewelry, etc.. Standing behind him was another guy who I think was his friend.

"I don't know you." I said

"Yeah, I know you! Off the internet! Lil' church dude!" he said.

Lil' church dude? I mean I didn't have a problem being identified with church, but his tone was something between disrespectful and crazy. I asked myself, "Am I being PUNK'd right now? Where is Ashton Kutcher?" Thank You JESUS that I didn't respond that way, though. Because the next words out of his mouth were a turning point to my evening.

"Yeah, I straight enjoy that stuff you put on YouTube tho'. Like everybody be sharing it… But, I don't believe in God; but I dig your positivity, lil' dude."

Lil dude? REALLY! I thanked him reluctantly and walked off before I said the wrong thing. Then I felt God pulling me back. Telling me to go back and talk to the man although he was probably feeling the effects of a beverage...or two...or three. I tried to talk to God (like you know we do when we REALLY don't want to listen).

"Lord, YOU *KNOW* where I'm at mentally right now. I'll smack this dude!"

Needless to say, God won that argument (He always does). So I went back to the man and asked, "Hey bruh', explain to me WHAT God you don't believe in?"

I think I caught him off guard. He looked at me and asked what I meant. I said again, "Explain to me What God you don't believe in." After he thought about what I was asking,

He said…

"People believe God's gonna do everything and I feel like you have to do some things on your own."

I nodded in agreement adding, "Faith without works is dead."

He said…

"Growing up with my mama and the old folks, you couldn't do this or that…"

I nodded in agreement adding, "You can't put new wine in old wine skins."

I figured out from our discussion back and forth that he had a background in the church and that there was some hurt or pain there. He found out from our discussion back and forth that the same God he said he didn't believe in, I didn't believe in either. We came to an agreement, even laughing and speaking on a respectful level that was nothing like how our conversation began. Although I can't say he accepted Christ at that time, I do believe a seed was planted for him to receive Christ later. I saw him leaving in his VERY expensive luxury car later that night, and I was thankful that God gave me the opportunity to be there to speak to that man.

The thing that really hit me hardest after that night was that with all the nice clothes and jewelry and the expensive car... THIS WAS THE GUY THE LADIES WOULD CHOOSE! At this stage of his life he was hurt and rejected, and only wanted a relationship with himself and things that made him LOOK like he was whole when in fact he was incomplete. He was dealing with so many internal issues that he purchased things that made him appear to be bigger than he was. But...HE DID NOT BELIEVE IN GOD and he was hurting on the inside.

Ladies... I AM CONVINCED THAT A MAN WHO <u>CANNOT LEAD</u> YOU IN PRAYER <u>CANNOT LEAD</u> YOU IN LIFE!

Men... I AM CONVINCED THAT A MAN <u>WHO CANNOT BE LED</u> BY GOD <u>CANNOT LEAD</u> HIS MATE OR HIS FAMILY!

After meeting that young man at the Rickey Smiley event I realized that although I didn't have all the money, cars, and clothes, I did have the voice of God. I had learned how to kneel before God and now I was confident that I could stand before any man or woman! It was time to bring my wife into the promised land! This wouldn't come without a fight but I needed my queen by my side.

Family, if you have learned to hear the sweet and quiet voice of God you have accomplished the most important thing in life. This is your secret weapon that isn't a secret at all. People may have more money and more "things" but you have a power working on the inside of you that will cause you to gain everything you need in this season of your life. I have learned that "stuff" comes and goes but the love of God never changes. I'd heard Kirk Franklin say, "I'd rather have Jesus than silver and gold." and I thought he was crazy but now I see that if I have Jesus I have everything I need. If I desire him, silver and gold can come when he chooses to bless me in that manner.

If you are in a period of transition in your life, remember that your mate is not your enemy - the enemy is your enemy. You may think that he/she should just "get it" but they don't. It may take some time for your mate to understand what God is telling you. Think about all the mistakes, the wrong doings, the failures you've had in your life. He/she may have been through some of those with you and now all of a sudden, you've got an epiphany from God that what you are about to do is going to be great... Really? Be mindful and consider that your mate may be afraid, uncertain, and sometimes downright rebellious. You may say, "I thought out of all the people in the world YOU would get it!" But they don't. How important to you is it for your mate to get it? If that person is important to you, you'd better work your butt off to make sure they understand as best as you can. If you can recognize the love God gives you every day - that's the love that should be reciprocated in your relationship. Most people want to be a master of much but they don't perfect the small. It's a small thing to explain, it's a small thing to show a person what you mean, and it's a small thing to serve them until they see it. You can do this family.

I can still remember when I called my wife and told her, "Babe I don't have much right now, but I do have a vision and I now recognize the voice of God and I KNOW Atlanta is the place God wants us." She had questions...DEEP, PROBING QUESTIONS... because she is an auditor by trade. But after tears, fighting, and even her refusing to come for a while, she finally moved from St Louis to ATL into our 700-square foot apartment. The moment that she came this little space immediately felt like home. Now, everything I needed was in place. God, Family, and Business. Business was on the way and when business came, IT CAME!

SAY THIS THIS PRAYER WITH ME

Father, I honor my mate and all that You have put on the inside of them. I pray that You give me the words to say to represent the vision that You put on the inside of me. Father, soften her/his heart to hear your voice. I will not give up on them because You have not given up on me. I honor You for my vision and I honor You for working things out for my good. IN JESUS NAME! AMEN!!!

* * *

1. **Remember that the greatest person on earth is a person who serves**. If your vision is cloudy I want you to serve in your home, your home church, in your community, etc. God unlocks revelation through service. If you know what area you want to

work in serve in that area. Don't worry about getting paid. SERVE. If you serve, the better opportunity will come. KEEP SERVING EVEN WHEN PEOPLE SAY YOU'RE STUPID BECAUSE YOU'RE NOT GETTING PAID!

2. **If you are led by God you have the upper hand.** Learn to hear His voice. Don't let "things" lead you away from God's voice. Things come and go but God's love lasts forever!

3. **Your mate is not your enemy; the enemy is the enemy!**

Sometimes people say some strange things during this period. Don't let your mate's temporary insanity stop you from loving them through it all. One day they will see it and be grateful that you took this leap of faith!

Love you Family,
Willie Moore Jr. #FLATOUT

"A MAN WHO CANNOT BE LED BY GOD CANNOT LEAD HIS MATE OR HIS FAMILY!"

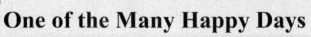

One of the Many Happy Days

IT WON'T ALWAYS BE LIKE THIS

Chapter 7

We had moved to Atlanta after losing our home to foreclosure and were living in the basement of my mother-in-law's home for a while. (Men, I really want you to dig in and get this, so let me break that down for you one more time…)

1. **FORECLOSED** on the REALLY nice 2500 square foot home that singing as Pretty Willie and working as Patricia Moore the auditor helped to buy.

2. Moved my **WIFE & CHILD** into the **BASEMENT of MY MOTHER-IN-LAW'S** home.

To lose your home and be evicted is a feeling that maybe only the people who have been through it can understand. Even if you haven't experienced this, you gotta know that it's a hurtful and discouraging thing. In our case, the fact that the home was a really nice open space in a beautiful neighborhood only added to the hurt.

In the city of St. Louis word got around quickly that "Pretty Willie" got foreclosed on. At the time, both myself and Patricia were wounded and in need of a place to begin healing. That place ended up being my mother-in-law's basement. Patricia's mother was nice enough to open up her home to us. She lived in a really nice home in a neighborhood, around "well to do" black people. Even the basement area we were staying in had its own space for a bedroom and a small bathroom. This was not my norm but it was a roof and a bed, and for the first time I really discovered what depression felt like. I can remember coming home from my office one day and a big Mack truck was in my lane coming directly at me, and I did not move. Luckily in the nick of time he must've realized he was in my lane and he moved. That's just how reckless I had become because of my depression.

I probably don't have to explain why this was tough for my wife. Women appreciate feeling secure. Especially when the source of that security is the man that they love and trust as their partner. For me though, moving into a 300 square foot space wasn't the tough part - going through that all I was internally struggling with was. My mother-in-law had a highly opinionated husband who found it amusing to keep asking me, "What you gon' do?" One day he ran into my mother somewhere and to this day my mother hasn't told me what he said but she was really ready for me to get out of that house. She refused to tell me what he said because I can have a bit of a temper when I feel disrespected and my mom didn't want me to go upside his head. My mother-in-law's husband really didn't want me to be there. Even though I had contributed $1000 to pay for us to stay there for a few months, he made it clear he wasn't happy with me staying. When God gave me the green light on moving to Atlanta, I was ready for a change.

When Tricia and I agreed to move to Atlanta, I was determined to do the right thing for God and the right thing for my family.

My rule #1 was to never be house broke.

For those of you who don't know what house broke means, it's when you live in such a nice home that the cost of the rent or mortgage plus expenses is above your means and puts you in a place where one unexpected bill could put you behind in your other payments. Too many of us are living this way...

I was not going to live above my means because I refused to do ministry to eat. I hate to see people in church begging for money... "Stand in this line if you have $1000... Stand in this line if you have $20." That has turned the "hood" off to church more than anything because many think church is all about the mighty dollar. I don't preach or minister to eat because I never want it to be about money. When we moved to Atlanta I wanted to make sure that the new place I chose for us to live was one where I could handle our expenses with my regular income on the internet and earnings from my live presentations. I went ahead of Patricia and my youngest son at the time and found a small apartment in Atlanta near the Greenbriar Mall area. Now, if you are unfamiliar with Atlanta's Greenbriar Mall it's a great area, however a lot of hustling and trapping goes on in the area in which we lived. The place was very nice on the inside, it's just that the outside was a little uhhhh, how do I say……. different. A lot of times to get to the inside of our apartment, you had to pass the dude smoking weed, the baby mama drama, the people fussing and cussing, and the loud music. But once you made it inside you could see how beautiful it really was.

I remember the day Patricia pulled up to our apartment for the first time. She had her mother with her and almost immediately was in tears. Not the good kind... She was pissed! She had this look on her face. (You know that look on a person's face when you just KNOW they were talking to people about a place they were going to... And then they get there and it's NOTHING like they thought- THAT FACE!) I can just remember her saying, "This… *cannot* be it". Her mama tried to play it cool and keep Patricia calm by letting her know, "You know, this is a good start." My mother-in-law is the sweetest woman in the whole world. She always has my back no matter what. Even if she doesn't totally understand what I am doing.

Even though my wife didn't intend on disappointing me, her words and facial expression had already caused me to puff up and fall into my prideful attitude and we had a huge falling out. I felt so bad at that moment that I said some really stupid, horrible things.

"Well you know there's an option… You can go back home!"

Now the truth was God had already told me that Patricia was supposed to be right there with me for every step of this new journey. I had no business saying anything that sounded like I would be fine with sending my wife away. Besides, she was leaving her secured nest of St. Louis to live with a man who had just lost his house to foreclosure. Did I mention that I had no job that paid money? I was serving in a ministry for free and I was depending on God to have people book me and people to watch my YouTube videos and sow into our T-Shirt wing of the Young Fly & Saved ministry. For me to say those horrible things was probably the worst thing I could do. I was just so mad at the fact that even though we weren't having to live in a basement anymore and finally had our own place again she was expressing disappointment. I remember looking into her eyes and beginning to calm down.

Then I prayed and God said in my spirit, "It won't always be like this... trust me." I believe what I had taken the time to pray for was key. I prayed:

"Lord, can You help me pass this test I'm in? Can You show me the way so I won't ever have to go through this test again?"

After that, God gave me a vision to share with my wife. A vision of the work that had to be done and the changes that we needed to make in our household and business. A vision that would set us up for the places we were headed. First, I began to post YouTube videos and put a schedule together to be consistent about it. I got Patricia involved. Then I began to write down all of the things I desired for the home we would have one day... The number of bedrooms... The mother-in-law suite... The room for my son to play in... etc. I got Patricia to come into agreement with me on the home. (*Seeing a pattern yet fellas?*) **Even though we were in this little apartment in the middle of a new place with little money, WE REFUSED TO STOP DREAMING HARD AND SETTING GOALS!!**

I repeated God's words to my wife, "*It won't always be like this... trust me.*" And I meant it. I took that time in the little apartment to dream with her and set goals with her. She really got involved with the process and when the time came to do the work we were on the same page. We knew what we wanted, but in order for us to not stay stuck in the place where we were, we needed a vision, a dream, and a goal for where we wanted to go. After prayer one day I gave my wife an update:

*"God is birthing something out of us, and just like any baby it takes nine months to grow and develop. Give me **nine months**... and I believe the Lord is going to do something **amazing**."*

Almost eight months had passed and after looking at so many houses in all areas of Metro Atlanta, none of them met our "dream" criteria. Many times my wife would say "why don't we just settle for this house." I wasn't having it. We wrote the vision of what we needed and I know God didn't give us these desires for nothing so I stood on my word. Now, you know that caused quite a bit of heated conversations but I was the leader and I knew that my wife was just in a rush to get out of that apartment! Time kept passing, and I was thinking to myself, "Wow, we're getting close..." Nothing was happening that looked "**amazing**". Keep in mind also that we were in a 12 month lease so not only would I need the money for the home we desired, but I would need money to break the lease for the apartment, at least that's what I thought. One day while I was at the apartment there was a horrible argument going on between a man and a woman, and I heard the whole thing. I mean this was some next level *baby mama drama*. Luckily my wife and son weren't there because this dude outside had a gun.

This fight was getting worse, and it was obvious he was about to do something really crazy. I had seen this man coming and going for about a month and had developed a rapport with him. I had always had good conversation with him, even seeing him angry before about other situations and encouraging him that he was bigger than his issues. I would talk to him about the love of Christ in a cool way and we had developed a mutual respect despite whatever disagreement was going on between him and her. On this day he was at his wits end and ready to take the fight to the next level. As I approached his car I saw the gun on the seat as she was outside loud mouthing him and I watched as he moved closer and closer towards the gun. I called him over to my car as I pretended to be going to my car to get something. He was away from the *baby momma drama* long enough to talk to me and for God to speak through me and calm him down so that he could handle the words she was saying without reacting the wrong way. He told me before driving off, "Thank you so much. If it wasn't for you I would've done something stupid." Following the argument, I had a talk with the leasing office that managed my apartment. Because of the dangerous situation and my concern for my family, they released me from my lease! FREE!

Now I had to find a house and we had only three weeks left to move. To complicate things more, in the middle of the three weeks I had to find the place, Patricia was committed to a makeup artists' event in St. Louis. I was on my own when it came down to crunch time in finding a new place for us to live. The good thing is we had our goals and vision written so I knew what I was looking for. With Patricia out of town, *AMAZING* happened. It was just two weeks before our move date and I found a house that met all of our criteria... at first. It was a little over the budget. After some negotiation they agreed to lower the price if I agreed to a longer lease, and I was able to get us in the home! In Atlanta after a foreclosure you usually have to wait a long time before you can rent again, but do you know the Lord found a way for that foreclosure not to come up in any of our application processes? WOW! It took all the money we saved up, but it was worth it! When Patricia returned from her trip and I was able to turn the corner onto our new street address it felt so good to see her face light up. The dream of our home was "birthed" right on time, as I gazed in my wife's timid, beautiful eyes when she asked "Really, is this my home?" and I was able to answer "Yes"... It was worth all the pain of that last year.

I gotta keep it 100 with you! It took another year for her to unpack everything in the new home. I know now it was because she was in constant disbelief of how God had blessed us in a huge,

huge way. We had stayed faithful to the vision God had given, worked to meet our goals, and walked in agreement towards the dream. After a two-year lease in the house guess what happened? We made the landlord an offer to buy the home and they accepted! We are homeowners again!

If you are in an uncomfortable situation it is important that you never stop dreaming together in your relationship. Drive around to neighborhoods you want to live in. Stop at an expensive hotel and walk around as a family so you all can dream. Don't get so bogged down with the immediate because you will miss the ultimate.

SAY THIS PRAYER WITH ME

"Father, we desire to dream again. I know that You have the power to change our situation at any-time You chose. Until then we pray for agreement and we pray that You would use us to dream the dreams You have designed for us. We know that You will give us the desires of our hearts. Please unlock our unknown desires and strengthen us with wisdom to accomplish all You have in store for us. IN JESUS NAME! AMEN

* * *

Enjoy the journey family,

Willie Moore Jr. #FLATOUT

PATRICIA'S TAKE

What can I say about our family's transition to Atlanta? Well for me Atlanta was always the party spot. The Black Mecca that I never took seriously because I kept hearing about over-crowdedness and "Freaknik!". My girlfriends and I would drive down to ATL all the time to party during our college days and then come right back home. Everyone I knew wanted to move there and me always wanting to be different and go against what's popular, I didn't ever want to move to "ATL Shawty". I however, knew that I didn't want to live the rest of my life in STL, but I definitely wasn't checking for Georgia. Therefore, after foreclosure and Willie mentioning to me a transition to ATL I immediately resisted it. I asked all kinds of questions like, "Are you sure?.. Did God tell you that?..Pray again and ask the Holy Spirit." LOL. I just knew something had to be off. Maybe it was a different place that started with an "A". Willie was serious though, so it looked like this would be the next phase of our life.

Now because I was hesitant to make that move, Willie went first to secure a place to live and scout out the land. That meant getting to know the place, learning the flow of it, and scanning the environment so that we could determine if this was truly where we were supposed to be. I wanted him to really have a peace about it. See, what you may or may not know is that we moved to California when we first got married. It was easier then to get up and leave STL and follow a dream, because we had done it before. However, you think differently when you have a kid involved. I was more cautious because I now had a son involved and I wasn't as willing to take those same risks like when it was just Willie and I. Children can change your whole perspective on life and well being. Peyton was in a really good school, I was starting off in my makeup career, and we had a great support system. For me a support system was truly instrumental at a time when our foundation crumbled and both of us were walking by faith, operating as entrepreneurs in our gifts. Usually, when there isn't a stable factor you don't just up and move to a new city. So for about a month I stayed in STL and prepared as much as I could for the move ahead (the unknown). Is that not an oxymoron?... LOL. Preparing for the *unknown*.

As I was in STL I tried to research and find schools for my Pre-K child to transition into. I was looking for a school that reminded me of the school he was already in. Researching online really didn't serve much justice. Both Willie and my mom told me I need to physically be in the city to find what I was looking for. Not finding a school was just another excuse I was making to not go to ATL. I was so set on just staying in STL and having Willie travel back and forth. I thought he could work in ATL during the week and come back on the weekends.

OK, so my stubborn self finally went. Let me say this. My "stubborn" is not the true definition of stubborn. That is a behavior that I've used to cover up my fear. I've never seen this done "in the natural realm" so it was really terrifying moving with nothing and taking your child. I'd heard about stepping out on faith, but now it was required of us to solely depend on God.

Willie made mention of my disposition upon arriving to ATL, which was not very pleasant. I remember getting off the exit from the highway and looking to the left. I saw Greenbriar Mall, a beauty college, Rainbow Fashions, a discount mall (flea market), a beauty supply store, and plenty of quick-loan money centers. What does that tell you? Yep, it's a good indication you're in the hood. I was thinking, "Where does my husband have us living?". I was born in the city of St. Louis and raised in the hood until the age of eight. My mom, as a single parent, told me she worked hard to move us out of the hood so that I could have opportunities that would potentially not take me back there, but here I was again. Now there is nothing wrong with the hood overall. However, if it's filled with violence, drugs, etc., it's not an environment I want to raise up a young son in. This is what was going through my mind and my face showed it. My face always shows what I'm thinking (I'm working on that). I was still processing everything and trying to take it in. No matter the circumstances, whether it's my mom's basement or an apartment in the hood, I know how to overcome and make anywhere a home. Initially my feelings try and take over, but then I bounce back and I don't operate in my feelings. It's important not to stay in your feelings! What seems like a bad situation could be worse based on your reactions and responses.

I will say the apartment was gorgeous on the inside. Within the gates it was actually a beautiful community. Once my husband and I settled in and discussed the vision, I realized we were about to accomplish something. Getting out of the boat and "walking on water." We were trusting God for everything and not one day did He disappoint. This move changed my faith, my mindset about God, and created a whole new relationship between us. I say the day I moved to Atlanta is when I was born again. There's nothing like living without your support system, not being able to rely on anyone, and not even being able to rely on yourself to provide (no job or safety net). It can be tough in the natural mind. We lived day to day off manna. You can't prepare for the unknown as mentioned above; you just have to do it. You have to believe God for His Word and the promises He made. It's about challenging that Word and watching it come to fruition. It's about being REBORN! It's the willingness to go into the unknown. Putting your guards, down petitioning your dreams to God, and allowing His will to be done.

**Moving Day...
Our New Home!!**

I AIN'T SLEEPING WIT NOBODY

Chapter 8

The strife from all of our disagreements and transitions had suddenly taken over our home and you could feel it. We were no longer communicating effectively, and to be quite honest we just didn't like each other anymore. If I said go left, she'd say go right, and if she said wheat bread I wanted white bread. It felt like an elementary school tug of war game. Nothing I could do for her was right and nothing that she did for me was right. Intimacy became a thing of the past. Now I know you think when it comes to most men they will RSVP to every sexual pass a woman throws, especially if it's been days, weeks, or months since you've had an encounter. I have even heard the old school saying "Ain't NO loving like NEW loving." For me that was not the case. I had developed a new mindset. I had learned my lesson from my past failures with women. I knew my worth, but this strife had caused my wife and I to no longer be intimate. Call me crazy, but I can't give you my loving if we ain't getting along. I know that some men are reading this and thinking "that doesn't matter", but to me it does. If I give you a part of me I literally have to be connected to you in more than just a physical way, I like intriguing conversation, a smile, a hug, and great energy between us. My wife and I were no longer connected other than the fact that we'd said "I do."

As we slept in our bed I can definitely remember an invisible line running down the middle of our queen size bed. That invisible line simply meant, you stay on your side of the bed and I'll stay on mine! This went on for a while and I finally found myself looking online one night. I don't know how it happened exactly, but I ended up falling into a porn site. Now as a kid we all had our share of peeking at dirty books and crazy late night Cinemax movies (AKA Skin-A-Max), but here I was a grown man on a porn site. I stayed a little too long and what do you know, I would visit these sites more and more often as time went on. Everything in me was saying, "This is not for you!" But I made excuse after excuse to justify it. When necessary, to make myself feel better about it I would tell myself, "At least I ain't sleepin' wit' nobody." In my mind I was only using these images to satisfy my instant sexual pleasure, minding my own business, and not hurting anyone else. Besides, I was watching to spark my sexual interest towards my wife again. Right? WRONG! I'mma Keep it 100! Fellas with all that airbrushed makeup and perfect angles from cameramen on porn, your wife will never live up to those fantasy images. And even if she could, do you want her to? Anyway… I digress.

Pornography had the complete opposite effect on me. My sexual feelings towards my wife started to dwindle away even more. Now, instead of sleeping with the invisible line in the bed I chose to sleep in the guest room. After becoming a Christian, I had worked to never be secretive about things plaguing me or hinder my growth as a leader. I always kept it real with my designated accountability partners. What in the world was happening to me? You only try to hide and keep secrets about your issues when you either want to keep doing them or when shame has overtaken you. Eventually, when you get tired enough, you will fight by praying and reading God's Word. Then pray some more. Then read some more. Finally, when it seems help is not coming, you *will* scream for help. By this time, I was screaming from the top of my lungs, HEEEEEELP!

It seemed like no one understood except for my dear friend Prophet Jermaine Greene. Up until that point, a lot of people I confided in told me to stop and pray on it. Others told me that they watched porn and it was ok. But Jermaine had a new interesting perspective on my porn issue. He assured me that God was still with me and he had a solution to my porn. He said if I liked it so much I should tape my wife and I having sex. What?!! Tape my wife and me??!!

"Yes", he said. "See, sex isn't bad. In fact, it's good when you do it the way God has ordained it", he explained. "Willie, you are taking in sexual pictures of someone else's daughter, someone else's wife... God's precious creatures who weren't designed for your eyes to see and take in those types of images. Your wife was designed for your eyes and if you are in need of a visual, record you and her."

What?!! A Prophet said this to me!

Then he said, "By the way, stop sleeping in the guest room. God wants you back in your bedroom."

Whoa! I almost passed out when he said that. I didn't tell him I had been sleeping in the other room. He *must've* seen in my eyes that I was uneasy. Right? I was *so* surprised that he knew that I wasn't sleeping in my marriage bed and had resorted to sleeping in our guest room.

He said "I know God just told me... Be well."

That had to be one of the *most* interesting encounters... *ever*.

Now before you scurry off to your local video store or site to purchase your favorite tripod and begin to tape your sexual encounters, please note on record that I did NOT take the prophet's advice. Although that may be good for some people, that information didn't fit our home. I liked the advice and it may help your relationship, but we were moving too much and I couldn't risk losing the tape in transition (I can't have a Willie Moore Jr. sex tape floating around the world. There are certain things that never need to be seen by anyone else but your mate). However, I took the second piece of advice to heart. I stopped sleeping in the other room, which helped stop me from being alone with the thoughts that caused me to fall into those sites. It's not good for man to be alone. To assist in what I coined my "wake up call" instead of goal oriented screen savers or fun stuff, I added my wife's face to everything. I added her face to every device I owned. Computers, studio monitors, cell phones, you name it… There was a picture of my queen. It was almost impossible to look in her eyes and go to the sites I wasn't supposed to be on.

After literally months of the tug of war, I was able to stop. I feel like I starved that desire by setting up boundaries for when my brain decided to go numb. Most people fool themselves into thinking that if the flesh doesn't rise up you don't want to fulfill that desire. LIE! The mind is a powerful tool that responds to what we feed our flesh. I knew that if I wanted to win the battle against porn I had to have boundaries for my body and my mind. Even when I traveled for three years, I kept someone in my room with me. I never traveled alone to any city… by any means. If you couldn't afford to bring my accountability partner, then I could not do the ministerial event. I have a desire to do the right thing, however this flesh of mine has a mind of his own sometimes; so when it decides to rise up over my natural will, I have guardrails set up so I don't run off the path.

After a while I came clean to my wife. This was tough to do because women often times think something is wrong with them. Fellas, if your wife preferred porn over you I'm sure you'd also feel a certain type of way. Even with your macho self, you would be hurt. I explained to her that it had nothing to do with her looks, her body type or her loving. It was totally just me being selfish and not taking on my rightful role of the "priest of the home". I was supposed to be implementing conversations that would get rid of the strife that was stopping us from being intimate in the first place. It had come to the point that I believed that I knew what she was going to say before she said it. The problem was that I was praying for change but I never mentally imagined nor did I believe what I was praying for would happen. This was evident because if you pray for a change you have to expect some things to change. How can you stop looking for your prayers to work if you have EXPECTATIONS? You can't!

She knew that she couldn't compete with these fake women on the computer and she refused to. And I wouldn't let her. **We made it our business to be upfront and talk about our struggles because you only keep private what you want to keep *to yourself*.** Including struggles and sufferings. You only get help when you get honest. When my eyes are getting reckless looking too hard at people who are not my wife I tell her, "Pray for my eye gate." If I find myself slipping backwards I am proactively upfront and honest with her so we can pray about these things and work together on a solution. This is my life partner and I attempt to give her all of me. The good, the bad, the victories, and the trials. She's my life *part-ner*, which means she takes *part* in everything I have.

SAY THIS PRAYER WITH ME

Father, I pray against the unhealthy habits that we have developed along the way. You said that in every temptation You give us a way of escape. I pray that I will see the way of escape and go that way. Holy Spirit guard my eye gates and help me to be intentional with what I watch. Father, I want to love what You love and hate what You hate. IN JESUS NAME! AMEN

* * *

1. **Add pictures of your mate on all your devices**. Look at him/her and look at all you have built together. Think of all the things you've had to endure together. Is it worth risking it all for and image?

2. **Be honest with your mate no matter how hard it is for him/her to understand.** Don't let your embarrassment stop you from getting your partner involved.

3. **Before you go into any porn sites pray about it.** Say God is this what you want me to do? If he says "YES", do it… But I'm sure He won't.

Love you family,
Willie Moore Jr. #FLATOUT

"THE MIND IS A POWERFUL TOOL THAT RESPONDS TO WHAT WE FEED OUR FLESH."

Patricia: Mommy, Makeup Mogul, & My Boo!

I HAVE DREAMS TOO

Chapter 9

The one thing about being a good example, staying disciplined, and staying true and strong on what you believe in, is that people notice what you are doing... especially your mate. Likewise, if you are a procrastinator and don't keep your word he/she notices that as well, so be careful. I am blessed to say that when it comes to focus and going after goals I don't lag in those areas. I personally don't even have to know all the information to get started and I don't fear many things. If it's something I want to do and I feel led to do it, I dive in head first. I come from Berkeley, Missouri and the streets taught me that *scared money don't make no money,* so I have no problem going for it.

My wife, on the other hand, is an auditor by trade. She needs to see a plan, know the risks, evaluate the threats, and the list goes on and on. This is really good for a business at some point, but as I've explained to her those things sometimes stop a person from getting started. It's too scary to know all the things that can go wrong when you are stepping out on faith. Now, I know people who are esteemed business school scholars are cringing at this information and I am sure your professors told you the whole spiel about business plans and securing funding before you get started… But I came from the hood. When you come from STL sometimes you don't have time to know all the "can't dos". Sometimes you have to count the cost and go for it!

After roughly eight years of our ministry's existence my wife had sacrificed a lot. She placed a lot of her goals on hold so I could achieve mine. This was really starting to take a toll on her and our family. I will keep it 100, sometimes I don't know how to comfort her in this. Even if I say the right thing it doesn't seem to resonate with her. If I say it at the wrong time I'm harsh and if I say it too passively I don't care enough. Ugh! This is my baby though, so I had to figure this out.

After saying things wrong on many occasions, I started seeking God on how to communicate what she needed to do to maximize her work/home balance. I wanted to teach her how to grind like a girl (Hmm… "Grind Like a Girl" sounds like a good book I should write. Anyway, back to what I was saying…). How could I communicate to her what a good work and home balance looked like? I know she would ask a lot of hard questions so I broke it down very simply. Grind like a girl means that she would learn to grind in the little nooks and crannies of her day. What may take someone one month to do might take her two or three because of the kids and home responsibilities, but she could still see a great return on her investment. Now, how could I get this information to a woman who is handling her business and still be sensitive to her feelings? She was used to working in Fortune 500 companies, receiving a high 5-figure salary and now she was feeling "reduced" to a stay-at-home mom. Ladies you may say, "I would love to not have to work 9-5" until you have to be with babies 24/7. Of course, this family was part of her dream too. Of course she loves being at home with the kids. But when you are used to working and going as you please, the transition can be tough to say the least.

I said a simple prayer that went something like this:

Father, I repent for everything in me that's not like You. I pray that You would give me the right words to say to my wife to motivate her, encourage her and inspire her to go for her dreams. Father, I pray that she would honor my voice in this matter. Father, guide me to voices that she honors in her life besides mine to give confirmation to seeds that You have planted through myself and others. IN JESUS NAME! AMEN

* * *

The moment I did this I began to hear her phone conversations differently, especially when she talked to her friends. It was almost like God was telling me "listen" to her while she talked to her friends. I could hear the difference between voices she felt authority over and the voices she honored. I realized I fell somewhere in the middle of those people. Instead of getting upset about my slot I prayed and waited for God to turn that thing around.

After numerous occasions on the phone with one of her friends I noticed that she listened attentively and I knew that I had identified a secure voice that she honored. In a cool way I asked her how she felt about this young lady (her friend) and she agreed that she respected her a lot. This young lady had two babies and worked as a stay at home mom. Her husband works as a performing musician and his job requires him to travel a lot. Her friend still managed to start school and work as a musician herself. I really think that intrigued my wife. I began to pray that God would use this lady to inspire my wife. See, most of us think that we have to be the only voice our mate honors. Not me. God used a donkey, a rock, and I *know* he can use a human being to speak into someone. Case in point, God's using me right now to speak into your life, and I am an outsider with an inside perspective to possibly empower your future.

This woman opened my wife up to the solution to her inner fight. Sometimes pride would tell me "that woman is saying the same thing you said." I would say "Get thee behind me Satan." I don't mind how my wife gets the information I just want her to get it. One plants the seed, another one waters the seed but God gives the increase. I am ok with that 100 percent! #FLATOUT

After a few months I started to notice a difference in her trajectory and the way she looked at herself. I began to bring flowers home every single week. I started to celebrate her instead of just tolerating her. If she cooked, I praised, if she cleaned, I praised, if she shaped her eyebrows up, I noticed. I have learned that the world beats up a woman so much with all these images of women with fake butts, fake careers, and fake lives, and that women take a lot of that stuff to heart. Fellas you have to do your best to combat the enemy by esteeming that woman in the highest regard.

My wife is now getting used to being a full-time mom and business woman. She loves makeup so we have started a makeup business where she freelances. She has worked with the likes of Tyler Perry, Black Girls Rock, and she is a personal makeup artist to a lot of Atlanta's up and coming celebrities. More recently, she has taken a liking to working out relentlessly. You know... I see an opportunity coming out of this, but I am being patient. Instead of trying to *make* something happen out of her, I am looking for voices that she may honor in the "work-out" space that can assist me in that area until she invites me into that space.

SAY THIS PRAYER WITH ME

Father, I know that I see the potential in my mate that he/she may not see in themselves. Father, I pray that You would soften my mates heart to hear what You are saying through me. Father, I pray that You would send voices of confirmation that he/she honors. I pray my mate is strengthened to capitalize on his/her vision and goals without distractions. Show me how to serve his/her wants and needs in this area. IN JESUS NAME! AMEN

* * *

PATRICIA'S TAKE

Dreams for me do look different than Willie's outlook. I'm more of a "reality" person (as he's mentioned) because of my upbringing and career choices. He's always been groomed to make it happen, focus on the goal and don't worry about anything else.For me it is a little bit different. Now when I was single I could make moves freely because I had no attachments or other people to care for. However, when you step into the wife and mom role you automatically put your family first and you become (unconsciously) last. Everything you think about is predicated upon the well-being of your family. After a while, you start noticing that you don't even make time for yourself because after serving the family you're too tired to do anything. It's a habit that's formed and it's almost as if you're in auto-pilot waking up every day doing similar tasks.

There are instances where I've felt like all I am is a mom. I know I have more in me! I know God gave me my own dreams and aspirations, but how do I fit that in my lifestyle? That's the question. Let's be honest, being a mom (or even a stay-at-home mom) is the most rewarding job ever; you're often the first to witness milestones, you're able to participate in all of your children's activities, and most of all you get to watch your little hearts outside of your body grow up. On the flip side, it's also the most challenging job because the family doesn't realize that they are selfish. They don't realize that they always need or want mommy. It's like second-nature, they just automatically call out "Momma!" However, mommy needs a break, time away to be an adult or just something outside of home. I used to feel like whenever I would plan something for myself there was always an obstacle or hurdle to prevent me from doing it. Therefore, I would stop planning stuff. I felt SO defeated. It was so hard to push through and get out of the house to go meet up with friends or even do makeup. Every time I would try and get ready the baby would cry non-stop, the other child wanted all of my attention or needed to finish homework and couldn't finish without asking me to help, or the husband would call asking me to help with something. When you're a stay at home mom your family is used to you being there all the time so if you're trying to leave it's like something triggers them and they go into "operation stop mommy" mode. LOL! They do everything they can to keep mommy home, bless their little hearts. After a while though, this can get discouraging and has kept me from trying in the past. See, with dads they can just go (well at least for some). If they want to work a thousand jobs and pursue a thousand dreams they have the security of knowing they can go freely because their spouse/mate will hold it down. For moms we have to find child care, cook the meals to make sure everyone eats right while we're gone, make sure homework will be completed, and basically, make sure the house will still function as normal. This takes a lot of brain power and moms as we know most of our exhaustion comes from how much we over-think situations. It's mainly because as I mentioned before, we are in the care-taker mindset and operating as career-goal-oriented go-getters comes second!

I didn't grow up with the example of a two-parent household or in a family where mom and dad were both risk-takers;

entrepreneurs balancing home and work. I basically have been winging it, through much prayer taking on each day as it's presented to me. However, I am a research junkie; I'm always seeking and looking for an example of someone to frame a picture for me of what family balance looks like. Not only what it looks like but what it looks like in a Godly household. I prayed for mentors. Our family dynamic is very unique; therefore, I needed wisdom and guidance from someone who could relate. Yes, God speaks through people and he sent me some great women of God who were willing to pour into me, share their stories and show me what it looks like for stay at home moms married to men who are either entrepreneurs, in ministry or both. Some women said they had to sacrifice a few years until it was time for them to step out into their calling. Others told me I may have to find something that lined up with my husband's vision, this would allow me to still have my own goal; however, it wouldn't take away from the family. These women were very adamant though about me making myself a priority. A happy mom results in a happy home!

I appreciated my husband for wanting to also step in and help me. We would sit and talk and brainstorm. Visions and goals would just roll so easily off his lips. He would say "ok you got it, now roll with it, get it done." I would sit there almost in tears because I'm thinking how am I going to get all of this done. He made it sound so easy; was he oblivious to all of the madness that goes on when I try and put my goals into action? However, we were looking at it from two different perspectives. He was looking at it like why can't you and I'm looking at it like how? This is another task on top of you, kids, home, bills (I manage home finances) and businesses. So I would take the plan to my new mentors/friends and they would explain it in a way that made sense; women know how to console each other and say the right things because they come from a place of understanding and compassion. My husband always meant well, he is a direct business man that has a very passionate heart. I couldn't force him to understand my feelings nor did I expect him to (it took time to get this way). I accepted that He is in the role he is supposed to be in, he is a visionary. Yes, do I want him to be a little softer and understand what it's like to be in my shoes; however, I am thankful God knows what we both need. Both of us honor the voice of God and nothing moves or compels us unless we know it's the Holy Spirit leading us. We are still growing and learning how to communicate and support each other; each phase of marriage requires new wisdom.

At this time, my thought process is that I have to get things done by any means necessary and that may mean without depending on my husband. He has his tasks and responsibilities which are very demanding; however, he is executing. I can't continue to let anything keep me from my God given destiny, I can't lose myself. I have to re-define myself and create a balance.

This mom won't stop at nothing to walk out her purpose and if that means waiting on God, sacrificing or even pushing through tough days, I will. I'm not alone in this walk, there are other women who have come before me and have been successful. God said He knows the plans for my life...Jeremiah 29:11. Therefore, I am encouraged. I will leave you with another scripture that's written on my mirror and I read daily:

Hebrews 10:35-36
So don't throw away your confidence — it brings a great reward. You need to endure so that you can receive the promises after you do God's will.

My "Good Thang"

TRIANGLE OFFENSE

Chapter 10

Towards the end of this book I think you'll have noticed a pattern. I have begun to talk to God before I talk to my wife. Nothing really long and deep; just a quick consultation with the Father insisting His will over my own. I, for one, am really tired of having to come back apologizing, enduring the silent treatment, and at times having intense conversations about my own lack of knowledge when it comes to the right timing to bring up things or just not knowing the correct approach to a tough subject. For the most part, I just keep it 100 and that can sometimes go wrong. So instead of coming back and asking God to fix it, I have learned to consult Him before I start. Now ladies, before you get all mushy or church-*ified* saying "awww" or "AMEN!", just know I have not mastered this principle yet, but I have named it. I call it the the Triangle Offense. This is a basketball term referring to a play that the L.A. Lakers started to use back in the early 2000's that they still use today. The Triangle Offense allowed every player on the offense to touch the ball causing the defense to have to scramble to know where the shot was going to be taken. Our triangle is a lot less complex when we are passing the ball because we are passing it to one person-GOD!

This "Triangle Offense" in a relationship is quite different from the basketball play. The triangle simply means that before I come to my mate with a problem or issue, I am going to consult with God first to see if it's the right time, to get the right approach and to see if this is a conversation that needs to be had in general. Instead of going to him/her blowing up and talking about how you "feel" I am asking you to go to God first and wait until you feel the peace and the timing needed to handle the issue.

One day on a quiet afternoon, we were sitting in the kitchen in our home in Georgia. Our son was in school, the sun was shining bright in our kitchen, and the timing seemed to be right to bring up some of our business issues to my wife. We have the ministry, a clothing line, and other businesses that we oversee. It takes a lot of communication. Working with my wife had always been a task to say the least, because we were still working on cutting off the husband/wife feelings to get some of our business conversations done. I had an issue about something she said in front of one of our team members, and the way she said it. Instead of tackling this problem head on, I decided not to bring it to her when it happened, but to try the "Triangle Offense" first. I prayed this prayer:

"Father, I repent! Please remove all anger that would cause me to sin. My wife has said something today that hurt me and I pray that You would not let strife come into our relationship. Father, You said, "For whoever would love life and see good days must keep their tongue from evil and their lips from deceitful speech." I want to love life and have a good day, so please reveal to me the root of this problem so I can speak to the root and not the symptom of my wife's agitation."

* * *

I waited for a while, walked upstairs and I began to have general conversation. I don't recall how we got on the subject, but I asked my wife a few family questions. "When you were young, what was it like growing up without a father in your home?" She began to say the things that I had heard before. "It was cool because my momma worked hard to provide. My family did… (YADA-YADA-YADA! I had heard it all before, but because I was running the Triangle Offense I heard it differently). For the first time in my life I heard the child in my wife. She sounded to be 11 years old repeating what someone had told her as a kid and not truly sharing how she really felt. I shut up and kept listening until she shared words that were now clearly engraved pains in her psyche from a young age. After she finished there was a brief pause and in a stern yet loving voice I said, "THAT WASN'T FAIR!" She broke into tears.

I told her that God showed me as she was talking a vision of an 11-year-old girl who was holding a teddy bear and wanting answers on why her father wasn't in her life like the other children she went to school with, but instead of getting direct answers she received explanations on why her mom worked so hard. Although I commend her mom for being the best mom she could be, I wanted my wife to feel the apology her heart desired for 30 plus years. She needed someone to fight for her and love her through and I was going to be just that. Thanks to God I discovered my position. I kept repeating "THAT WASN'T FAIR". I held her close as she sobbed and wept like that 11-year-old child on my shoulder. As I felt her warm tears on my shoulder, I rubbed her head and told her that it was ok. I assured her that it wasn't fair and I vowed that I would do whatever it took to help her grow from this. The conversation and the tears went on for about an hour straight. We discussed why it was hard for her to take constructive criticism and through "The Triangle" God gave us strategy. The problem was that she still had authority issues, but the solution started when I ran the "Triangle Offense". God revealed the root of the problem and didn't allow me to get hung up on the symptom. Today if I give my wife constructive criticism in front of others and her emotional side can't take it, instead of defending herself we have a secret sign we use for her to tell me she is not feeling my tone. It's simply two fingers that look like antennas or bunny ears over her head. It translates "talk to me softer" because she is feeling like that 11-year-old girl. I then quickly change my approach to one that is more gentle, and I even hold her in my arms embracing her heart until she's comforted. I thank God we are getting stronger together in this area. The antennas happen less and less nowadays as God is removing all of our past hurts. #FLATOUT

Wooo! Breathe! That was deep, but it doesn't have to be. My wife now uses the "Triangle Offense" for little issues like when she wants me to clean the kitchen or picking up my socks, and she says it works. I'm serious though. No matter what your issue or problem is, before you bring it to your mate make sure you bring it to the manufacturer of your mate. God desires to give you clues on the root of the problem and insight on how he wants to dissolve it forever! So many people divorce over issues from their symptoms of deep dark rooted problems, but God, through the Holy Spirit, desires to give us the right timing and the right atmosphere to tackle these issues at the root so we don't have to fight on the surface.

We all have scars in our lives that shape our thinking and trigger our reactions. I challenge you to care about your mate enough to explore all parts of them. Enjoy the good and bad and consult with God so you two can uproot every issue that plagues you in your current relationship. It may be a past hurt from a previous relationship. Maybe it's a family issue or simply an unhealthy view of yourself hindering you from being the best version of yourself. Whatever it is, you have to be willing to help each other through every part of it. Only you know what your "it" is, but share it with your mate.

Alone you have one head, two hands, and two legs. Together you have two heads, four hands, and four legs. This makes it so much easier to defeat the enemy. You are better together!

Love you,
Willie Moore Jr. #FLATOUT

"WE ALL HAVE SCARS IN OUR LIVES THAT SHAPE OUR THINKING AND TRIGGER OUR REACTIONS. CARE ENOUGH TO EXPLORE THEIR SCARS."

We Go Together

WE MADE IT

Chapter 11

What do you do after the struggle is over? What do you do when your vision comes to pass? Well, the process is never over… You just get better! Your foundation has to stay grounded in God through Jesus Christ. Pride has a way of trying to make you believe that you are the source of your success. Don't take the bait and don't fall into the trap! Check this out:

Now that we are in a beautiful home, making enough money to pay tithes, save, pay the bills, sow seeds into several ministries and take vacations a few times a year, things are really cool. Our crazy vision of making videos and encouraging a nation of people is really coming to pass and paying off. My wife doesn't have to go to work 9 to 5 for anyone but she has the hardest job in the house… raising our boys. In our vision while we were "going through" I can remember her dropping off Peyton to daycare when he was just a few months old. He was our first baby together as a married couple and that morning she cried like a baby. She loved the daycare but the thought of someone else having her baby after the 6 to 8 weeks she had been home nursing him hurt her heart. She said her goal was to stay at home and raise the kids. I took that to heart, wrote it down, prayed over her desires, and asked God to provide for this request to come true. Guess what? He provided for this desire to come true. This should be enough for a woman to relax, hush, chill and cheer her man on every minute of his life right? WRONG!

Although I know my wife is extremely proud of our success she still has a habit of complaining about little things. "Pick your socks up... Did you leave the refrigerator open? ... When are you going to take the kids for a while so I can rest?" In my male opinion, if I am keeping the lights on and you don't have to leave the house to work for anyone besides yourself, then the least you can do is not nitpick me. *I* provided the life you ask for, *I* take care of the bills, *I* try to spend as much time with you as possible, I -I -I -I -I. Have you noticed a trend here? I -I -I. *I*'s will always make you feel unappreciated.

In the first paragraph I explained to you that while I was on my way up I wrote down her desires, prayed over them, and GOD provided. Now that you are living in the blessing it is so easy for us to think that we did it. The moment that you put yourself in the center of the equation YOU LOSE! See, my wife hasn't changed she *always* told me to pick my socks up, she *always* wants me to close the refrigerator, and *everybody* needs a break from kids, but when you look at what you are doing for the home it's easy to become selfish. Now, ladies I am not saying that you can't have a small cup of shut up or be quiet but fellas I am reminding you that she is the weaker vessel according to the Bible. Whatever you do that your mate doesn't see God sees and you will receive your reward in heaven. I know that may not be good enough for your flesh so this is what I have learned to think about when I need to feel appreciated or if I get overwhelmed. LISTEN!

Recently I took a job on the radio as a nationally syndicated radio host. In all honesty, this is my first corporate job. I have always had my own business and despite all of the ups and downs, through Christ, I know how to make it! When this opportunity came to us we were really excited, we counted the cost and how much time it would take away from my main focus, HOME! After much prayer along with weighing the pros and cons, we took the opportunity. Now understand, no one can truly prepare you for such a big platform. The calls, the appearances, the opportunities, the practice, the show preps, etc. Not to mention that I still have a ministry that requires me to catch a flight every weekend, a clothing company, two television shows on TBN, a show on the BET Network, a publishing company and a record consulting business. Can you say WOO-O-O SA-A-H. The radio opportunity was great; however, we couldn't count what we couldn't see. After about six months into the job working at night, I was moved to afternoon drive time. More people, more pay, more pressure.

This was the first time on the inspirational format they have ever syndicated an afternoon show. Our founder, Ms. Cathy Hughes, is a beautiful soul. However, she likes to win and many people were depending on me. I thought I had explained the responsibility well to my family. However, when I would come home after work my wife would continue the same ol' same. Willie comes home, gets the kids and she can go relax. It was cool but I could now feel the pressure and I needed to take a break before I could click into daddy mode. I explained this to her but the same behavior kept happening. Instead of consulting God on the matter and using the Triangle Offense I made a stupid, stupid mistake. I BLEW UP AT MY WIFE! One night we were having an intense conversation, to say the least. We were talking about our responsibilities and I felt like she didn't understand the pressure I was under nor did she care. In the heat of the battle I said "put up or shut up!" I literally told her if she wasn't going to put any money in the bank to take care of this family, BE QUIET! This is a wound that she will never be able to forget. Although, I felt what I said was true I didn't mean to say it that way. She was nagging me so hard and I was trying to explain to her in this "learning season" that we needed to implement a new system in our home until God revealed to me how to navigate through this new responsibility. But I said it *WRONG*.

That night instead of apologizing I let the sun go down on my wrath! I went upstairs and laid down until I noticed the baby was crying. I was wondering when she was going to pick him up or something. I heard the garage go up but I figured she'd left something in the car. I went to his room and picked up the baby, then I checked on my middle child and he was sound asleep. Our home is pretty big so I checked all 3 floors and I couldn't find my wife. I looked outside and wouldn't you know it… the car was gone. My wife had left the house! I called once to check on her and, of course, she didn't answer. I put the baby to sleep and instead of letting my imagination go crazy on where she could be, or what she could be doing. I began to repent and cry out to God.

The prayer sounded like this:

Father, I repent, I said some wrong things tonight and You know I didn't represent You the way I should have. Please forgive me. Now Father, talk to your daughter like only You can. Let her know that I meant no harm in my words. Soften her heart, let her come home safely and better than she was before she left. Forgive me Father. IN JESUS NAME! AMEN

* * *

Normally, I would keep calling, texting and I would let the devil play with my mind. After all these years I finally discovered that God is omnipresent, meaning that He is everywhere. He never sleeps or slumbers so you know what that means. TO SLEEP I WENT. In less than an hour after the prayer I heard the alarm "beep-beep" indication that the door was opening and she was home. I am not sure if she slept in our room that night but I knew she was in our safe house and for that I gave God praise.

The next morning, I woke up with a renewed mindset and amazingly, my wife wasn't giving me attitude. I began to think. "What the heck is wrong with her." She cooked breakfast and was being nice. I thought to myself "This woman is trying to kill me." I asked her where she went last night. She said she drove to a nearby parking lot and talked to a family friend and her friend explained to her what I was going through and how she had to depend on God to change my heart. As I calculated time, almost at the exact same time I was praying that night Patricia was being ministered to by our mutual friend. God was changing us both. I apologized for my words and she apologized for not hearing my heart and we have become stronger from our debacle.

I want you to know that what you think will change your relationship for the better will actually challenge your relationship for the worst if you are not careful. Most people believe that once you get money and stability all the relationship woes go away. LIE! On every level you two will still be becoming one flesh. As long as you notice how "I's" are rooted in pride and the key is getting your focus off "I" and on bringing God's glory through your relationship. God desires to be in the center. Ladies, if your focus is to serve him and his focus is to serve you (after God) you two have your relationship moving in the right direction. Of course, ladies it will always feel like a double standard because you have to be all things to the home but I want you to be comforted. We can't do it without you boo. Fellas, find a way to make her feel appreciated. It doesn't have to cost money, send her a text and say:

Babe, I love you and I appreciate everything you do for us.

Boy, you might get *blessed* when you go home if you're married. If you're not married don't you go over to her house after that!

SAY THIS PRAYER WITH ME

Father, I repent. I know that none of my successes could have happened without You. You are the source of my increase and because of that You will be the chief navigator of how to handle the season we are in. I will keep You in the middle and when I am tempted to think I am in the center of my success, Father please reveal it to me and I will check myself so you don't have to. Father, I love you so much. Teach me how to love my mate the way he/she is designed to be loved. You made them so I'll follow your lead. IN JESUS NAME! AMEN

* * *

Love you,

Willie Moore Jr. #FLATOUT

"WHAT YOU THINK WILL CHANGE YOUR RELATIONSHIP FOR THE BETTER OR CHANGE YOUR RELATIONSHIP FOR THE WORST."

 **In The Beginning…**

ON THE HIGHWAY

Chapter 12

My prayer is that you have read something that has changed your mind about the things you've had to endure in your relationship. I trust and believe that everything you have endured is all part of a bigger plan that God has for you. I know you have heard that far too many times, but take it from me it is part of a bigger plan. You may not understand why you have to endure so much, but in the end it will be clear. You know the old saying... "Hindsight is 20/20." You were made for more than what you see now and in order to sustain the place where God is taking you, you have to develop the character that is needed. My favorite book says, "The just shall live by faith". This means as long as you are living, it's going to take faith to keep moving in the direction God wants you to go. Maybe you have given up on your relationship and you picked up this book not really looking for a solution, but you have found one for your relationship. Maybe you are in a healthy fruitful relationship and you just needed to fine tune some things. Maybe you are single, and you are looking for the right information before you get into a relationship. I pray that you received what you were looking for and that you have learned some valuable lessons for what's to come. I believe that one of these stories was your story and you said, "Wow, they went through that too". I believe that some of the characteristics in us made you think long and hard about some things that you can fix for the sake of your relationship. I am so blessed to say that we made it through, and because God's grace is on every single one of us, you can make it too. Who cares about the past?! We all have a past, but we don't have to be prisoners to our past.

The great Willie Moore Sr. (my father) says, (and I quote:)

"If you find two people who agree on everything, either one of them is crazy or both of them are crazy!"

I thank God for that information because it means that you are not going to agree on everything, and it's ok to disagree without being disagreeable. One last story, and I am going to let you go, I promise.

It was late one afternoon in St. Louis in 2005 and my business partner and I were riding clean in my gold 1999 4-door Mercedes Benz E430. The sun was shining and we were in a great mood because I had finally finished my album "The Transition" and it was time to mix the album with the great Adam Long. To my musically uninformed people "mixing" means that we were going to fine tune the sound of the record. Got it? GOOD. We were about to travel 47 miles out to Eureka, Missouri to hang out in Adam's exclusive home studio where he boasts the best ears in the Midwest. When it comes to mixing songs, I must say I agree that he's one of the best in the business, so it was worth the trip. As we rode with the tires shined up you couldn't help but notice the cars riding by looking at two young successful black men riding in a Mercedes with their fitted St. Louis Cardinal baseball hats on. Boy, did it feel good to be almost finished with my first independent album. After a tough deal with Universal Records I decided that the independent route was best for me.

As we rode down 270 (the interstate in the St. Louis area) I was in the passenger seat of my car while my partner drove. Alongside of us we noticed something (Someone actually!). She was so fine that it made us both look twice.

My friend said, "She's eyeing you Bro". I told him she had to be eyeing him because "I'm riding *scrub*" (Scrub is a popular term from a TLC song called "No Scrubs". In the chorus of the song it says *"I don't want no scrubs, a scrub is a guy that can't get no love from me. Riding in the passenger side of his best friend's ride trying to holla at me."*). I fit the "scrub" description that day, but this young lady looked very familiar to me. As she looked and I looked we caught eyes and I mouthed to her, "Don't I know you?"

I kindly asked her to pull over by pointing my finger to the exit sign and she obliged. I hopped out of the car and I really thought I knew her from somewhere. It was like we had met in another life before. We later realized we'd met in passing from the many college parties that we both attended. I asked her name and she said, "Patricia".

"Well Ms. Patricia I'm going to call you sometime. Can I have your number?"

She gave me the digits! This was before text messages became the most common way to communicate. I was in the middle of finishing my album, so it took me a week or two to call, but one night I called her and we immediately clicked. We ended up talking for hours and hours and we really had a connection. She went to church, she grew up in the hood, she loved God (and cussed a lil bit) and I did too. Wow! What a connection. For many weeks we just talked on the phone without any real visits. I can recall meeting her at a restaurant with her friends one time, but nothing too intimate with just us alone. Patricia was truly my friend. In fact, I became so comfortable with her that we used to talk about my dating issues. One young lady I was dating at the time used to wear the same belt every time we went out. I got so tired of that belt. I told Tricia, "If she wears that same belt one more time it's over between us!" We laughed so hard and later that weekend I called Tricia to let her know the young lady and I were finished. "Why?" she asked. "The girl wore that belt again!" (I was so trivial back in those days). We also talked about my relationship with the mother of my child. I was also in the middle of trying to stay with the mother of my child for the sake of my son. Patricia was such a champion for me to stay with her for the sake of the child because of all the things she had been through growing up, but I knew that my child's mother and I were better off as friends raising a child the best way we could apart from a husband/wife relationship.

One day, I asked Patricia if I could stop by her house and she obliged. When I arrived at her condominium I was so surprised to see that this young lady had her stuff together. Her home was decorated nicely, and it was so-o-o-o clean. I had dated ladies who could not keep a home this clean if they had a housekeeper, but this woman did it all by herself. I was a young homeowner and she was a young homeowner. We had so much to talk about in that regard. After a while she visited my condo as well. Would you believe I bought the condo she had really wanted? She said it was a little out of her price range. Talk about coincidence! I remember the day I visited her condo, she had on some black pants. Now, I had never noticed her body because I was so intrigued by her mind and her opinion that I must've overlooked those hips. Today was different because I noticed. I mean I really noticed. As we talked more and more, I realized that she was everything I wanted in a woman. I was known as a "player", but I was ready to let all that go because of this woman. She accepted all of me. With all of my many attitudes and quirky ways she just laughed and loved me. I desired for her to be free in her own skin around me as well. She didn't have to do all the girly-girl stuff if she didn't feel comfortable. She could just be fun, happy, silly, smart, cool, hood (yet classy) Patricia. She was my queen and I knew I had to make it official.

I'm not sure if I ever asked her to be my girlfriend, but it was just understood that we cared for each other and exclusivity was around the corner. I began to make the announcement to my many "friends" around the country that I was seeing someone and things were starting to get serious. I asked a lot of them not to call my phone after a certain time and many of them got the hint that this relationship meant something to me. One young lady threatened to tell Patricia about all the crazy things I was into. What she didn't understand is that I'd talked to Patricia about everything. Some people were angry and tried to hinder what we were developing, but I feel like God shielded my wife and I from the bulk of the hate. After only a year of dating, I knew that I didn't want to spend my life with anyone else. The truth is, I didn't fully understand what a husband was, but just like everything I do, I don't have to have the full information to make a decision. I felt that tug from God and I got on one knee and asked her for her hand in marriage.

I think she said yes. All I remember is a lot of screaming and hollering in the house.

See, Patricia grew up in University City. That's a town about 12 miles away from my hometown of Berkeley. Her mom was just about to move into another home at the time. Tricia grew up in this home and all of the memories she had there were about to be only engraved in her mind, because the house was already sold and they were just waiting for the closing day. I walked in during the going away party and waited until the family was around and I said, "You started your dating here and I want it to end right here as well." I got on one knee and I popped the question, "Will You Marry Me?" Her aunt Vernice tackled me! Evidently she said yes because we have now been married for eleven years. I was so happy and scared at the same time. I knew myself and I didn't want to wait years before we tied the knot. I was interested in getting married soon because we had decided to live together after our engagement and I wanted to be right in the sight of God. We got married in three short months, and 11 years later we are still going strong. Today we have three children: Khalil Benjamin Author Moore is our oldest (he is 14), Peyton Micah Moore is our middle child (8 years old), and the newest edition to our Kingdom is Princeton William Moore.

It's so funny how we met and how this awesome story began. Every chapter of our life has not been a walk in the park, but in every season we became stronger together. We heard the negative talk from some of our peers, friends and loved ones, but if the opinion of people didn't line up with the word of God we paid it no mind and did what we knew to do as a Christian couple. Are some things out of our control? Yes! But we don't focus on that. We focus on the things that we are in control of. Like communicating even when we don't feel like it and setting boundaries for our family when the world desires to keep us busy. We decided never to go to bed with any unforgiveness in our hearts and mind. Even if we don't come up with the solution that night we talk about it and pray about it, and even if we agree to disagree God has a way of mending the broken pieces. All because we attempt to do what God has called us to do.

My heart goes out to you for all the things you've had to endure in life and in your relationship. Believe me, I know that everyone has a story and yours is unique in its own right, however remember that if someone else had the same cards you were dealt in life they would be winning right now.

Don't miss this...

If someone was dealt the same cards you were dealt right now they would win with those cards.

You're angry because you can't buy groceries for a party, while someone is looking for their next meal. You're upset because you can't take a vacation, while someone needs a home for their family. You're mad because he isn't working, but he's looking for a job daily. Someone has a man who desires to work but due to physical ailment they can never work again. You're upset because she gained some weight while someone is having to take their wife to dialysis right now and wishing she could have the healthy weight your wife has.

Family, YOU have an opportunity today to be grateful! Every day of your life I want you to thank God that he chose YOU for this opportunity. The opportunity to serve another person every day of your life, because we get a glimpse of what it's like to be God in a sense. All the shortcomings, all the hurtful words, the mistakes, and the mishaps... They are all opportunities. We get a chance to love someone through it all. JUST LIKE GOD LOVES US.

All in all family, my prayer is that you would not give up. No matter what. The storybooks usually end by saying, "AND THEY LIVED HAPPILY EVER AFTER." That is totally not the case in our marriages and relationships. If I had to best sum up our story and yours ... "AND THEY LIVED HAPPILY AFTER ALL!

LOVE YOU!
Willie Moore Jr. #FLATOUT

PATRICIA'S FAREWELL

As you have read, being married can pose challenges! The responsibilities, requirements, and expectations are a lot for one person to juggle, especially when you add in the roles of being a father/mother or husband/wife. You find yourself with a full calendar and no time left for what means the most to you. Quality time with the ones you love. Because you are either so focused on a mission or goal, or perhaps the problems and stresses of life, your loved ones get your leftovers. Don't get me wrong, it is a blessing to be a blessing to others and most importantly to operate in your gifts, so you should be spending time doing that. However, you have to set up boundaries or you will get drained very quickly. Prayerfully, the ones who love you will be standing beside you and holding you up with understanding hearts and patience, praying for God to fill up what's been poured out and to cover the family so there are no feelings of separation and loneliness.

With great rewards come even greater responsibilities! We want God to "enlarge our territories" and provide stability within our lives, but with it comes some heavy loads to carry. It's so easy to get caught up in ourselves, our visions and careers and not realize how much precious time has passed. I'm not telling anyone not to buckle down, focus and press hard until you meet the mark. What I'm saying is, if you want to achieve "Happily After All" in your life you must be willing to put in as much work into your relationship as you would anything else you're passionate about:

1. **Establish a healthy balance.** Therefore, discuss and define balance based on your family's dynamic. Implement a workable solution that will make everyone happy. If you have to, set dates to do it and give your loved ones something to look forward to.

2. **Keep the Relationship Fresh!!** My favorite reminder of this is, "He who finds a wife finds a good thing and obtains favor from the Lord."

Make sure that you are being courted ladies. See, in the beginning it was customary for the man to chase or pursue the woman. Once you get married, have kids and pursue your dreams, the courting seems to dwindle away. Fellas, women always love a chase, a date night; to be wooed and romanced. Ladies allow your man to be the man and make you feel special. Sometimes we may need to remind them of the things we love and that make us happy. Guys, if you don't know how to be romantic, like anything else you are serious about... Study it! Read books, watch some good romantic flicks; be intentional about keeping the fire and romance in the marriage!

By now I pray our transparency has answered the questions of, "What now?.. Could my marriage work?.. Does it get better as time progresses?" If you're anything like me, after reading a good self-help testimonial type book, you are praying that it will work and things will get better. You should be on fire because you made the effort to read a book about how God is working through others like you. Two imperfect people. Get ready to put all the suggested tools into action. Let me just say there is no perfect relationship or 100% correct way to navigate through the ups and downs of marriage. There wasn't a lot of tangible examples when we got married because what happened in marriage stayed behind closed doors. People weren't as transparent with sharing their stories and experiences. Yes, Willie and I knew some great couples and we appreciate their gifts of wisdom along the way. But our marriage was designed, created and very uniquely made for us. We had to put in our own work. What I've realized is that God has a great sense of humor and knows how to keep us praying.

I love you all and I pray that you took at least one thing away that ministers to your soul and gives you hope. Besides, isn't that what we all strive for? To be HAPPY and HOPEFUL after all we've overcome!!!

Sincerely,
Patrica Moore

MESSAGE FROM THE MOORE'S

Every time you think of us we want you to pray for us. Pray that God would continue to strengthen us a family unit. We are working to be a blessing to one another, and a blessing to the body of Christ. We are not perfect people, but we serve a perfect God, and through his son Jesus we are made perfect in the sight of Father God. I know that's deep for some. That simply means through Jesus our shortcomings are covered. What an awesome liberty to go through so much and have God still use us in such a capacity as this.

Please keep our relationship in prayer, as our overall goal is to strengthen households and push our God-given agenda of getting kids currently in foster care adoptive parents or have good foster parents granted total parental rights. Keep us lifted in this mission.

If you are interested in foster care or adoption, please visit:

WillieMooreJr.Org/AdoptionIsAnOption

ABOUT THE AUTHOR

Willie Moore Jr. is a husband, father, nationally syndicated radio host, television personality, highly sought after conference speaker, music publisher, Grammy recognized songwriter, and author with a following of over one million people.

The St. Louis native uses his gifts to inspire people, positively influence the world, and glorify God always. Willie now resides in Atlanta with his wife Patricia and sons Khalil, Peyton, and Princeton.

Willie is the son of Willie Moore Sr. and Flora Moore who adopted Willie at the tender age of three months. Willie has been quoted as saying "After God, all that I am I owe it to Willie Moore Sr. and Flora Moore." With a heart for adoption awareness Willie's "WILFLO FOUNDATION" has raised awareness about adoption and foster care children around the globe. The goal of his foundation is to establish healthy homes for all children and to provide scholarships to foster children and adopted children.

WillieMooreJr.org

CPSIA information can be obtained
at www.ICGtesting.com
Printed in the USA
LVOW13s0704140317
527007LV00012BA/66/P